LA CUISINE CAJUN

La Cuisine Cajun

Jude W. Theriot

PELICAN PUBLISHING COMPANY
Gretna 1990

First printing, 1986
First hardcover printing, 1990

Library of Congress Cataloging-in-Publication Data
Theriot, Jude W.
  La cuisine cajun.

  In English.
  Includes index.
  1. Cookery, American—Louisiana style. I. Title.
TX715.T383   1986   641.59763   86-774
ISBN 0-88289-806-X

Manufactured in the United States of America

Published by Pelican Publishing Company, Inc.
1101 Monroe Street, Gretna, Louisiana 70053

To Nicholas Luc Theriot and Edna Materne Theriot, my Acadian grandparents. Paw-Paw had a love of the land that always made me respect him. He also raised every kind of animal and vegetable needed to produce great kitchen delicacies. He gave me my knowledge of fresh vegetables and fresh meats. His sense of humor was always intact. He had a gentle firmness and a great love of his grandkids. Maw-Maw was a quiet, unobtrusive woman. It was easy to feel the great love that came from her gentle heart. She was also a great cook. Both Paw-Paw and Maw-Maw enjoyed the fruits of the land and worked hard, but they always got what they needed from the farm they cared for. For me, going to "the country" to visit them was always a treat and an educational experience. I hope my book serves to give both of them back just some of what they gave to me through the years.

And Nicole Marie Theriot, my daughter. She has been the high point of my life. She is so full of spirit and life. Her positive attitude and ability to turn dark moments into happy ones are qualities that make her a delight to have around. To her my love forever.

Contents

LA CUISINE CAJUN

Introduction

La Cuisine Cajun is first of all a Cajun cookbook. The recipes are all solid and easy to use. No attempt was made to make them low calorie in the first place; however, many are. As it turned out, more than 135 of the recipes have fewer than 400 calories per serving. I have also given revised recipes for many higher-calorie dishes that will change the dishes somewhat but still keep taste as a focal point while offering a lower calorie count.

Writing a Cajun cookbook is no small task to undertake. I had to wrestle with questions like: What is Cajun cooking? How do you know if a recipe is really Cajun? Why is the Cajun way best? Which cooking methods are Cajun and which are not? What is the difference between Cajun cooking and Creole cooking?

My first feeling was to go with only the old traditional fare like gumbo, sauce piquante, dirty rice, boudin, étouffée, fricassé, bisque, jambalaya, and courtbouillon. These were all true Cajun dishes created over 100 years ago and representing the taste and culture of the Cajun people. As I began researching recipes, mainly by talking with respected and authentic Cajun cooks, I found one and only one thing to always be consistent: an inborn creativity that lives in the hearts of Cajun cooks. Their philosophy is, Do what feels right; use what you have and make it taste tempting. If you don't have fresh crawfish to make an étouffée, then make a shrimp étouffée!

I found that there were as many variations for all of the traditional Cajun recipes as there were Cajun cooks. I couldn't say which of the recipes were the "right" ones; they were all fabulous! I then examined my own cooking techniques and recipes, trying to remember what my grandmother had told me. I realized that I didn't always use the same étouffée, gumbo, or sauce piquante recipe. It depended on what ingredients I had and how my personal tastes were running on any given day.

As a result, this Cajun cookbook attempts to capture the Cajun flair for creativity. By no means do I expect it to be the last word on Cajun cooking, nor would I want it to be. My recipes are numerous and varied, and I've attempted to include my own personal favorites here. The traditional recipes are all fine-tuned composites of all of the tasting and talking that I've done while looking for the best of Cajun cooking. The ideas are culled from many Cajun cooks, from my grandmother's input, and from my personal preferences. I hope you'll use this book as a starting point. Try a recipe as it is printed first. If you like it as is, note that in the margin. If something comes to mind while you are cooking, then by all means give it a try! Be creative; make my recipes your recipes. Be sure to write your ideas down in the margin so you can duplicate the dish consistently in the future.

You'll also find recipes in this book that I've included because I happen to like the dishes or ingredients. They were experiments that I feel were successful. Use them as they are, or subtract or add as you wish. It is important to create dishes that you like and are proud of. Once you've done that, the chances are good that others will share in your joy and feast on the fruits of your cooking labors.

Louisiana Cajun cooking is not difficult. It combines a lot of ingredients to create a dish that is a melting pot of flavors. Look at the directions of a recipe to tell if it is difficult. Never let a long list of ingredients scare you away; remember, you only get back what you put in! It is the blending of flavors that makes Cajun cooking such a tempting treat.

My sincere hope is that after trying a few recipes, you will come to realize that Cajun cooking is not something to be feared, but rather a new experience in cooking that will broaden your areas of competence in the culinary arts. May La Cuisine Cajun allow you not only to eat like a Cajun but feel like one too!

The Cajun Story

Wherever I go across the country, people ask me, "Just what is a Cajun?" The word *Cajun* is a corruption of *Acadian*. The Acadians were the French people living in old *Acadie* (now Nova Scotia) who were expelled forcibly from Canada by the British in the 1750s and 1760s. Of all Louisianians of French origin, the Cajuns are just a part. Not all people living in Louisiana are Cajuns. The term should only be applied to the descendants of those Acadians who were driven from Canada.

That era was a terrible time for my ancestors. They had gone to Canada seeking a new and better life—free land, the ability to live as they chose, and the freedom to practice their religion. Their reasons for coming to North America were all valid and were soon all realized. They etched out an existence that was comfortable for them, but by no means lavish. They were hard workers and earned all they had by the sweat of their brows. The society they formed bothered no one, and they generally kept to themselves. Happenings in the American Colonies didn't concern them, nor did the war between Britain and France. Building hope and a future for their children was their goal and their priority.

As the world political situation deteriorated, the Acadians were faced with a crisis. The treaty that ended the war gave Acadie to England, and the British demanded that the Acadians swear a loyalty oath to the King of England and the Anglican Church. The French crown held no special place in the Acadians' hearts or lives, but they were French people. Their religion was very important to them; they were Catholic and would not consider any other religion. To these proud Acadians, such a loyalty oath was incomprehensible. Giving up their property and all earthly possessions, as tragic as it was, was their only option.

The British Empire was not satisfied with this peaceful settlement. They took an even crueler approach in expelling the Acadians. Families were deliberately split—husband from wife, mother from child, brother from sister, all shipped off to various ports and destinations. Many families were never again united. The agony that the British caused was never to be forgiven or forgotten. It became a part of the Cajun soul. Never again would a Cajun completely trust government, politics, or the opinions of outsiders.

Cajun settlements were set up all across the Atlantic seaboard and inland as well. Most Cajuns eventually made their way to Louisiana, where the French had settled 100 years earlier. So, Cajuns were not the first French in Louisiana. Some tried the life in New Orleans and attempted to assimilate into the New Orleans Creole way of life. For the most part, that did not work; they were not the same people. The Cajuns' culture had remained close to the French Provincial way of life of the early 1600s. In Canada they adjusted their ways, took some ideas, but their language and lifestyle remained those of 17th-century France. The ways of the Creole French were as foreign to them as were the ways of the American colonists.

Most of the Cajuns, then, went to the bayou country of Southwest Louisiana. There they developed a closed culture that cut them off from the outside world. Their own world developed separately from the rest of the state and country. Geography helped; there was no way to travel through the area except by bayou or a few very poor trails. Therefore they learned to depend on their families and on close, trusted neighbors. In addition, their experiences in the past with outsiders, foreign countries, and non-Cajuns had not been rewarding, to say the least. They trusted only each other. They could depend only on each other. Their way of life continued and was nurtured by the lavish bayou systems of Southern Louisiana.

No longer was their life cruel. They now had very fertile land, an excellent climate, a long growing season, and above all an abundance of fresh food (seafood, game, and meat). Perhaps the physical conditions of the bayou country kept them from becoming well-to-do, but the bayous also provided rich culinary delights. Dishes fit for royalty were everyday fare. Food was a commodity all had in abundance. In style, the cooking had French roots but developed into a unique form because of the availability of new foods and spices.

Cajun cooking is a unique blend of fresh ingredients, pungent spices, and creativity. It is as unique as each of its practitioners. The land created within the Cajun people a love of food and an ability to cook from the soul, not just from the pot. As a people we can draw from a varied background: France, Canada, Creole New Orleans, and our own Bayou Country. Cajun cooking is exciting, yet simple and basic. Let your palate be your guide. To cook like a Cajun is to live a little closer to heaven on earth!

The Theriots:
One Cajun Family's Ancestry

Jude W. Theriot
Born: 1947
    Lake Charles, La.

Wife: Deborah Patricia LeBlanc
Born: 1951
    Lafayette, La.

Fred L. Theriot, Sr.
Born: 1921
    Moss Bluff, La.

Wife: Mary Louise Borel
Born: 1922
    Lake Charles, La.

Nicholas Luc Theriot
Born: 1879
    St. Martinville, La.

Wife: Edna Materne
Born: 1882
    Baton Rouge, La.

Omar (Homer) Theriot
Born: 1850
    St. Martinville, La.

Wife: Josephine Jackson
Born: 1846
    St. Martinville, La.

Etienne Theriot
Born: 1819
    St. Martinville, La.

Wife: Julie Pouponne Picard
Born: 1826
    St. Martinville, La.

Joseph Theriot
Born: 1775
    St. Jacques (St. James),
    La.

Wife: Eulalie Rosalie Dupuis

Thomas Theriot   Wife: Marie Agnes Daigle
Born: 1743
    Grand-Pre, Province
    of Acadie, Canada
(Thomas arrived in the United States from Acadie with his mother, brothers, and sisters after being expelled by the British)

Joseph Terriot   Wife: Françoise Melancon
Born: 1699
    Port-Royal, Province
    of Acadie, Canada

Pierre Terriot   Wife: Marie Bourg
Born: 1671
    Port-Royal, Province
    of Acadie, Canada

Germain Terriau   Wife: Andree Brun
Born: 1646   Born: 1647
    Port-Royal, Province
    of Acadie, Canada
(Listed in the census of old Acadie taken in 1671)

Jean Terriau   Wife: Perrine Breau
Born: 1601   Born: 1611
    Martaize, Province of
    Vienne, France
(Listed in the census of old Acadie taken in 1671; Jean arrived in Acadie from France in 1637)

Gumbos, Soups, and Salads

CHICKEN STOCK

1 4½- to 5-pound stewing chicken
1 gallon of water
2 stalks of celery, cleaned
1 large yellow onion, cut into fourths
½ bunch of parsley with stems on, washed
2 cloves of garlic, unpeeled
2 tender young carrots, washed
2 green onions, washed, roots removed
2 bay leaves
½ tsp. of thyme
1 tsp. of sweet basil
12 whole black peppercorns
1½ tsp. of salt
1 whole clove
½ tsp. of Tabasco sauce

Wash the chicken well in cold water. Remove as much of the skin as possible and place the chicken (whole) into a large stockpot or gumbo pot. Add the water and bring to a boil over high heat. Once the pot begins to boil, reduce the heat to low and add all the remaining ingredients. Cover the pot well and let it simmer for 3½ hours.

Remove from the heat and lift the chicken out of the pot. When the chicken is cool enough, remove most of the meat from the bones and return the bones to the stockpot. Set aside the chicken meat for use in another dish, such as chicken salad. Return the stockpot to the heat and simmer the stock for 2 more hours, tightly covered. Remove from heat and let it cool enough for you to handle it, then strain the bones and vegetables out of the liquid.

Refrigerate the stock for 6 hours, then skim the fat and foam off the top. You should get about 2 quarts of excellent stock. This may be eaten as is, or you can use it as a soup or sauce base.

Lagniappe: Homemade stock is hard to beat! The making of the stock is not really hard at all; it just takes time. Make it on a day that you are doing something else away from the kitchen. Then you can either refrigerate the stock for use up to 4 days later or freeze it for use at a much later date.

To use, just let the stock thaw in the refrigerator and use as you would any fresh stock or broth. Only about 23 calories per cup, so you are adding great flavor with very few calories.

BEEF STOCK

5 pounds of beef soup meat
3 pounds of beef long ribs
1 gallon of water
1 stalk of celery, chopped
1 small onion, chopped
1 clove of garlic, minced
4 carrots, chopped
2 bay leaves, crushed

¼ bunch of parsley with
  stems on, washed
½ cup of chopped green
  onion tops
1 tbsp. of chopped cabbage
1 tsp. of salt
6 whole black peppercorns
½ tsp. of sweet basil
½ tsp. of Tabasco sauce

Preheat the oven to 500 degrees. Chop the soup meat into small pieces and set aside. Place the beef ribs in a shallow baking pan and bake them until they are quite brown but not burnt, about 20 minutes. Turn the ribs after 10 minutes.

While the ribs are browning, sauté the soup meat over medium heat in a medium (about 2-gallon-size) gumbo pot until it is well browned. Do not let the meat stick. When the meat is browned, add the water and bring to a hard boil. When the liquid is boiling, add the rest of the ingredients and reduce the heat to a low simmer. Add the browned ribs to the stockpot and simmer for 4 to 6 hours. Should the level of the water fall below the soup meat and ribs, add enough water to cover and lower the heat more.

When the simmering time is up, remove from the heat and let the stock cool. Strain the cooled broth through a fine sieve and place the broth in the refrigerator to chill. The fat should rise to the top and harden somewhat. Remove as much of the fat as possible. This should make about 2 quarts of excellent stock. It may be eaten as is or used as a base for other soups or sauces.

Lagniappe: You can make this stock ahead of time and store it in the refrigerator for up to 4 days or put it into airtight containers (canning jars are excellent if you allow room for the soup to expand) and freeze it for a few months. Let the stock thaw at room temperature and use as you would any broth.

Don't toss out the leftover meat from the broth pot. Even though the bulk of the flavor has been removed, you can chop the meat finely (it is very tender) and use it mixed with potatoes to make excellent hash. You can also season it up with barbecue sauce and make nice Sloppy Joes. Only about 31 calories per cup; a great way to liven up any dish with very few calories added.

SEAFOOD GUMBO

1 cup of cooking oil
1 cup of all-purpose flour
2 large yellow onions, chopped
1 cup of minced celery
⅔ cup of chopped bell pepper
3 cloves of garlic, minced
1 15-ounce can of stewed tomatoes
1 8-ounce can of tomato sauce
2¼ quarts of Seafood Stock (see index for recipe) or water
2 bay leaves
½ tsp. of sweet basil
⅛ tsp. of thyme
½ tsp. of Tabasco sauce
1½ tsp. of salt
½ tsp. of black pepper

½ tsp. of garlic powder
1 tsp. of onion powder
¼ tsp. of white pepper
1 tbsp. of Worcestershire sauce
2 pounds of okra, washed and cut into 1-inch circles
3 tbsp. of cooking oil
½ tsp. of salt
1 dozen whole crabs, cleaned
2 pounds of shrimp, peeled and deveined
2 cups of oysters with liquor
½ cup of finely chopped green onion
½ cup of finely chopped fresh parsley
salt and pepper to taste
filé powder to taste
cooked white rice

In a heavy metal pot, heat the cup of cooking oil over medium heat. Add the flour and cook until you get a reddish-brown roux. Remember to stir constantly. When the desired color is reached, add the onions, celery, bell pepper, and garlic and sauté for 7 minutes. Then add the tomatoes, saving the juice in the can for later use.

Sauté the tomatoes for 5 minutes, then add the juice from the tomatoes and the tomato sauce. Cook for 3 minutes, then add the Seafood Stock, bay leaves, sweet basil, thyme, Tabasco sauce, salt, black pepper, garlic powder, onion powder, white pepper, and Worcestershire sauce and bring to a boil. Once the dish has come to a boil, reduce to a low simmer and cook the gumbo for 1½ hours, covered.

In a heavy metal pot that has a lid, combine the okra and the 3 tablespoons of cooking oil, cover, and bake in a 375-degree oven for 35 minutes, stirring 4 times during the baking process. The okra should be cooking while the gumbo is simmering. When the okra is ready, add it to the simmering gumbo and replace the cover. Add the crabs, cover pot, and cook for 15 more minutes. Add the shrimp and cook for 15 minutes at a low simmer. Add the oysters, green onions, and parsley and cook at low simmer for 10 more minutes.

Check seasoning and adjust salt and pepper to your taste. Pour into individual serving bowls and add the filé powder and cooked white rice. Serves 8 to 10.

Lagniappe: May be made in advance and refrigerated or frozen for later use without any harm to the dish. If you do not like okra, you can leave it out. You can also vary the kinds of seafood to suit your taste. Serve with plenty of hot French bread and potato salad. About 495 calories in each of 10 servings or 618 in each of 8 servings. Add 112 calories per serving for ½ cup of cooked white rice.

CRAWFISH GUMBO

¾ cup of cooking oil
1 cup of all-purpose flour
2 large onions, chopped
2 stalks of celery, chopped
2 cloves of garlic, minced
1 medium bell pepper, chopped
1 15-ounce can of stewed tomatoes
3 quarts of hot water
2 tsp. of salt
1 tsp. of black pepper
¼ tsp. of cayenne pepper
¼ tsp. of Tabasco sauce
1 bay leaf
¼ tsp. of sweet basil
1 tbsp. of Worcestershire sauce
3 pounds of crawfish tails, peeled and deveined
½ cup of finely chopped green onion
¼ cup of minced fresh parsley
salt and pepper to taste
cooked white rice
filé powder to taste

In a very heavy gumbo pot or large, heavy saucepot, heat the oil over medium heat for 4 minutes, then add the flour. Cook over medium heat, stirring constantly, until the roux turns dark brown. When the desired color is reached, add the onions, celery, garlic, and bell pepper and sauté the vegetables in the roux for 5 minutes. Add the stewed tomatoes and sauté for 5 more minutes, then slowly add the hot water. Stir until the roux is dissolved.

Add the salt, black pepper, cayenne pepper, Tabasco sauce, bay leaf, sweet basil, and Worcestershire sauce and stir well. Bring the mixture to a boil, then reduce the heat to a rolling simmer and cook for 1 hour. Add the crawfish tails and reduce the heat to a low simmer. Cook for 25 minutes over low heat until the crawfish are tender. Add the green onion and parsley.

Check seasoning and add salt and pepper to your taste. Serve hot in individual serving bowls with filé powder over cooked white rice. Serves 8 to 10.

Lagniappe: This is an excellent dish to make in advance and either refrigerate or freeze for later use. It actually improves the dish to make it at least 1 day in advance. To reheat, just thaw in the refrigerator if frozen and heat over low heat until the gumbo is hot. Use this recipe to make an excellent **Shrimp Gumbo** by substituting shrimp for crawfish.

About 325 calories per serving in 10 servings without rice. With ½ cup of cooked rice there are about 437 calories per serving. In 8 servings there are about 405 calories without rice or 517 calories with rice.

CHICKEN AND OKRA GUMBO

¾ cup of cooking oil
¾ cup of all-purpose flour
2 large yellow onions, chopped
1 large bell pepper, chopped
4 cloves of garlic, minced
2 stalks of celery, minced
1 hen (6½ to 7 pounds), cut into serving pieces and most of skin removed
2 tsp. of Chicken Seasoning Mix (see index for recipe)
2¾ quarts of Chicken Stock (see index for recipe), chicken broth, or water
¾ pound of tasso (smoked beef)
1 bay leaf

¼ tsp. of sweet basil
¼ tsp. of garlic powder
¼ tsp. of onion powder
⅛ tsp. of white pepper
¼ tsp. of cayenne pepper
½ tsp. of freshly ground black pepper
¼ tsp. of Tabasco sauce
1½ tsp. of salt
2½ cups of smothered okra
1 tsp. of filé powder
¾ cup of chopped green onion
¼ cup of minced fresh parsley
filé powder to taste
cooked white rice

In a gumbo pot or large stockpot (2½ to 3 gallons), heat the cooking oil over high heat until the oil begins to smoke. Add the flour and stir constantly with a wire whisk or wooden spoon, making sure that the roux is constantly moving and not sticking in any part of the pot. (I find that tilting the pot from one side to another helps.) Continue to cook over high heat until the roux becomes a dark reddish-brown. This will take about 3 minutes.

When the desired color is reached, add the onions, bell pepper, garlic, and celery. Sauté over medium heat in the roux for 2 minutes, stirring constantly. Season the chicken with the Chicken Seasoning Mix. Fry half of the chicken in the roux mixture over medium heat for 5 minutes, then remove that half and fry the other half for 5 minutes.

Put all the chicken back into the pot and add the Chicken Stock. Stir until the roux is absorbed into the stock. Add the tasso, bay leaf, sweet basil, garlic powder, onion powder, white pepper, cayenne pepper, black pepper, Tabasco sauce, and salt. Heat over medium heat until the gumbo comes to a boil, then reduce the heat to low. Simmer for 1½ hours, then add the smothered okra and the teaspoon of filé powder and continue to cook at a low simmer for 2½ more hours.

Add the green onions and parsley and stir them in well. Cook for 7 more minutes at a low simmer. Serve hot in individual serving bowls with filé powder over cooked white rice. Serves 10.

Lagniappe: This is Cajun cooking at its best. Gumbo is one of the mainstays of the Cajun people. It can be made a day in advance and put in the refrigerator. This not only doesn't hurt it; it actually seems to improve the flavor. The gumbo will keep in the refrigerator up to 4 days. It also freezes well. To reheat, just thaw in the refrigerator and heat the amount you are planning to eat over low heat until it comes to the temperature you like. Add filé powder to taste and serve over cooked white rice.

To make **Chicken and Andouille Gumbo,** just follow the recipe as above except substitute andouille sausage for the tasso. Andouille sausage is a very spicy Cajun sausage, and it really lends itself to a gumbo. (If you cannot find tasso, beef jerky is an acceptable substitute.)

About 782 calories per serving of the gumbo without rice and 894 calories with ½ cup of rice. While this seems like a lot of calories, it is not when you consider that gumbo over rice is a complete one-dish meal for under 900 calories. I would not suggest making any changes in the recipe to reduce the calories.

DUCK GUMBO

¾ cup of cooking oil
1¼ cup of all-purpose flour
2 large yellow onions,
  chopped
1 medium bell pepper,
  chopped
1½ cups of chopped celery
3 cloves of garlic, minced
1½ tsp. of salt
½ tsp. of black pepper
¼ tsp. of cayenne pepper
¼ tsp. of white pepper
½ tsp. of Tabasco sauce
4 wild ducks, cut into
  fourths

2 pounds of pure pork
  smoked sausage, sliced
  1 inch thick
3¼ quarts of hot water
8 boiled eggs, peeled
½ tsp. of sweet basil
1 bay leaf
1 cup of finely chopped
  green onion
½ cup of minced fresh
  parsley
filé powder to taste
cooked white rice

In a heavy gumbo pot, heat the cooking oil over medium heat until hot, then add the flour, stirring constantly. Cook until the roux turns a dark, dark brown. Add the onions, bell pepper, celery, and garlic and sauté until the vegetables are soft, about 10 minutes. Add the salt, black pepper, cayenne pepper, white pepper, Tabasco sauce, and ducks. Cook over medium heat for 15 minutes, stirring constantly. Add the sausage and continue to cook for 10 more minutes.

Add the hot water and stir until the roux has dissolved. Bring to a boil, then reduce the heat to a low simmer and add the peeled boiled eggs, sweet basil, and bay leaf. Let the gumbo simmer over low heat for 2 hours, stirring a few times every hour. Add the green onion and parsley and cook for 10 more minutes. Skim off any excess fat. Serve hot in individual serving bowls with filé powder over cooked white rice. Serves 8 to 10.

Lagniappe: May be made in advance and frozen or refrigerated for later use. The flavor is not hurt at all by either process. To reheat, just thaw in the refrigerator if frozen, then heat over low heat.

You can use this same recipe to make **Blackbird Gumbo;** just substitute 16 blackbirds for the 4 wild ducks. Do not cut the blackbirds in half; let them remain whole. About 761 calories per serving in 10 servings or 951 calories per serving in 8 servings. Add about 112 calories if you serve each bowl of gumbo with ½ cup of cooked white rice.

CROCK POT BEAN SOUP

1¼ cup of dry white beans
1 ham hock
1 cup of chopped ham
1 stalk of celery, finely minced
1 small onion, minced
1 clove of garlic, finely minced
¼ cup of minced bell pepper
1 bay leaf

2 tbsp. of minced fresh parsley
¼ cup of chopped green onion
1 tsp. of salt
½ tsp. of Tabasco sauce
1 tbsp. of Worcestershire sauce
3 tbsp. of chopped cabbage
7 cups of cold water

Put all ingredients into a crock pot set on low. Cook for at least 8 hours or until beans are tender. Mash some of the beans with a heavy spoon after the soup is cooked. Stir in the mashed beans to change the color and thickness of the soup. Serve as a main dish or as an appetizer. Serves about 6.

Lagniappe: Why make this in advance? It is just a pour-it-in, turn-it-on-and-leave-it-all-day dish. It does refrigerate well after it is made and can be frozen, but the dish is so simple that I would suggest serving it at once. You can use any type of beans you like or even substitute dried peas. A hearty, filling soup. About 363 calories per serving.

FRENCH ONION SOUP

4 large yellow onions
2 tbsp. of butter
1 tbsp. of olive oil
1 tbsp. of minced celery
¼ cup of minced green
   onion bottoms
1 tbsp. of all-purpose flour
1 tsp. of sugar
1 quart of Beef Stock (see
   index for recipe) or beef
   broth
¼ tsp. of Tabasco sauce

¼ tsp. of freshly ground
   black pepper
¼ tsp. of white pepper
salt to taste
4 slices of French bread
   (about ½ inch thick),
   lightly toasted
1 cup of grated Gruyère
   cheese
4 tbsp. of grated Parmesan
   cheese

Peel onions and finely chop 2 of them. Cut the other 2 onions into thin slices; cut all the slices of 1 in half and separate the slices of the other into rings. In a heavy saucepan over medium heat, mix the butter and olive oil. Sauté the onions for 3 minutes, then add the celery and green onion. Continue to sauté until the onions begin to brown. Add the flour and cook until the flour is light brown. Add the sugar and Beef Stock and stir until the flour is absorbed. Add the Tabasco sauce, black pepper, white pepper, and salt to taste.

Let the soup simmer over very low heat for 20 minutes, then pour into individual soup bowls. Float a slice of French bread on top of each serving and cover each slice of bread with ¼ cup of Gruyère cheese and 1 tablespoon of Parmesan cheese. Bake for about 15 minutes at 375 degrees. Serve hot right from the oven. Serves 4.

Lagniappe: You can make this soup in advance; just don't add the French bread or the cheeses. You can refrigerate the soup for up to 3 days before serving. The flavor will be excellent. To reheat, just follow the steps above, starting with pouring out the individual servings. Do not freeze this soup; it has a tendency to lose its taste and texture.

    About 348 calories per serving. To reduce the calories considerably and still keep the great taste, cut the Gruyère cheese out completely and just cover the French bread with the Parmesan cheese. This will give you about 248 calories per serving.

POTATO-ALMOND SOUP

3 large white Irish potatoes
water to cover potatoes
salt
¼ cup of unsalted butter
½ cup of finely chopped
    green onion (bottoms only)
2 tbsp. of minced celery
½ tsp. of Tabasco sauce
1 tsp. of salt
1 tbsp. of Worcestershire
    sauce
½ tsp. of white pepper

¼ tsp. of onion powder
3 cups of milk
2 cups of half-and-half
¾ cup of toasted almonds
½ tsp. of Accent
1 cup of heavy cream
4 cups of Chicken Stock (see
    index for recipe) or
    chicken broth
minced green onion tops for
    garnish

Wash the potatoes and place them in a large saucepan. Cover them with cold water and lightly salt the water. Boil until the potatoes are tender. In a large heavy saucepan over medium heat, melt the butter. Sauté the onion and celery until the onions are clear, about 5 minutes. Add the Tabasco sauce, salt, Worcestershire sauce, white pepper, onion powder, and milk. Heat over medium heat, stirring constantly, until the milk begins to scald. Remove from heat.

Peel the cooked potatoes and dice them into small pieces. Add them to the scalded milk mixture, then add the half-and-half. Cook until the mixture is smooth, about 10 minutes. Remove from heat and let cool slightly. Pour this mixture into a blender or food processor and add the toasted almonds. Blend until smooth. Add the Accent and heavy cream. Blend for 1 minute.

Pour the mixture into a large saucepan and add the Chicken Stock. Heat, stirring constantly, until the mixture is hot but not boiling. Serve hot, garnished with the minced green onion tops. Serves 8.

Lagniappe: When I was executive chef at Le Champignon Restaurant in Lakes Charles, Louisiana, this was my customers' favorite soup. It is a wonderful soup. You can make it in advance and store it in the refrigerator until you are ready to use it. Heat it over low heat or in the microwave. Be sure to stir it well before heating, for it does tend to separate when left standing for any period of time. Do not freeze. About 495 calories per serving.

CREAM OF FRESH SPINACH SOUP

1 pound of fresh spinach
cold water to cover spinach
3 cups of Chicken Stock (see index for recipe) or chicken broth
3 tbsp. of butter
½ cup of chopped onion
1½ tbsp. of minced celery
2 tbsp. of all-purpose flour

3 large egg yolks, slightly beaten
¾ cup of heavy cream
½ tsp. of salt
½ tsp. of Tabasco sauce
¼ tsp. of freshly ground black pepper
¼ tsp. of white pepper

Wash and chop the spinach. Place it in a heavy pot (about 2 quarts) and cover with cold water. Place the pot over medium heat and bring the water to a boil. When the water starts to boil, reduce the heat to low and let the spinach simmer, covered, for 15 minutes. Add the Chicken Stock and simmer for 5 minutes, then remove from heat and allow to cool.

In a small skillet over medium heat, melt the butter and sauté the onion and celery for 5 minutes. Add the flour and cook for 2 minutes. Add this light roux to the soup base and stir in well. Put the mixture into a blender and blend for 2 minutes at high speed or until all the spinach is chopped fine. (You may use a food processor, but be sure that the liquid will not leak out of the bottom.)

When the soup is well blended, return it to the large pot and bring it to a boil. It should thicken somewhat. Beat the egg yolks and heavy cream together well. Add some of the hot soup base to the egg-cream mixture until the mixture becomes quite hot. Reduce the soup base heat to a low simmer and add the egg-cream mixture. Add the salt, Tabasco sauce, black pepper, and white pepper and stir well. Let the soup get hot again, but do *not* let it boil. Serve hot. Serves 6.

Lagniappe: A great cream soup—not really heavy, but thick enough to be quite nice. You can do a lot with this recipe; for instance, you can substitute any number of vegetables to make the kind of cream soup you want. Use asparagus and it becomes **Cream** of Fresh Asparagus Soup. Use yellow squash and it becomes Cream of Fresh Yellow Squash Soup. Use carrots and it becomes Cream of Fresh Carrot Soup. Use zucchini and it becomes Cream of Fresh Zucchini Soup. Use fresh leeks and it becomes Cream of Fresh Leek Soup. Use broccoli and it becomes Cream of Fresh Broccoli Soup. I could go on and on, but these are the ones that I have personally kitchen-tested. All you do is substitute 1 pound of fresh vegetable for the spinach.

This soup can be made in advance and stored in the refrigerator. Do not freeze it, though. It will keep for 4 or 5 days in the refrigerator; just stir it through (it might separate slightly during storage) and heat it up, but do not let it boil! The spinach version has about 226 calories per serving; the asparagus, 222 calories; the squash, 226; the carrot, 230; the zucchini, 224; the leek, 232; and the broccoli, about 226 calories. All are low in calories, but high in flavor!

HOMEMADE VEGETABLE SOUP

1 soup bone
3½ pounds of soup meat
1 gallon of cold water
1 14- to 15-ounce can of stewed tomatoes
3 stalks of celery, chopped into bite-size pieces
4 carrots, cut into 1-inch pieces
1 large onion, chopped
2 medium turnips, diced
1½ cups of chopped cabbage
2 cups of green beans, chopped into 1¼-inch pieces
1 cup of fresh corn, scraped off the cob (2 ears)

15 small whole new potatoes or 2 peeled and diced large potatoes
½ cup of chopped fresh parsley
¼ cup of chopped green onion tops
2 cloves of garlic, finely minced
½ tsp. of Tabasco sauce
¼ tsp. of white pepper
½ tsp. of freshly ground black pepper
2 bay leaves
½ tsp. of sweet basil
salt to taste

In the oven, broil the soup bone for 12 minutes on each side. When you start the second side, add the soup meat and broil it for 4 minutes on each side. Place the soup bone and soup meat in a large soup pot or stockpot and cover with the gallon of water. Bring the water to a boil, then reduce to a low simmer and cook the bone and meat for 1 hour.

Add the stewed tomatoes, celery, carrots, onion, and turnips. Cover and cook for 1 hour. Add the cabbage, green beans, corn, potatoes, parsley, green onion tops, and garlic. Cover and cook for 30 minutes. Add the remaining ingredients, cover, and cook for 30 minutes. Remove the soup bone and cook for 20 more minutes. Serve hot. Serves 10 to 12.

Lagniappe: To scrape the corn off the cob, stand the ear of corn on end and scrape the kernels off from the middle to the bottom of the ear with a downward motion all around, then repeat for the other end of the ear.

This can be made in advance and either frozen or refrigerated for later use. To reheat, just thaw in the refrigerator if frozen, then heat on top of the stove until it reaches serving temperature. It is really great to make this soup when vegetables are fresh and plentiful. About 430 calories per serving in 10 servings and 359 calories per serving in 12 servings.

CAJUN TURTLE SOUP

3 pounds of turtle meat
1½ tsp. of Seafood
  Seasoning Mix (see index
  for recipe)
3 tbsp. of peanut oil
3 quarts of water
2 carrots
¼ bunch of parsley
1 bay leaf
1 stalk of celery
3 tbsp. of flour
2 medium onions, chopped
2 stalks of celery, chopped
2 tbsp. of finely minced
  carrots
¾ cup of chopped bell
  pepper
1 tsp. of minced garlic
1 cup of tomato purée
1 cup of Beef Stock (see
  index for recipe) or beef
  broth

3 tbsp. of fresh lemon juice
1½ tbsp. of Worcestershire
  sauce
¼ tsp. of Tabasco sauce
3 bay leaves
1 tsp. of sweet basil
¼ tsp. of thyme
½ tsp. of black pepper
¼ tsp. of white pepper
½ tsp. of garlic powder
1 tsp. of onion powder
½ cup of sherry
salt to taste
½ cup of minced fresh
  parsley
2 hard-boiled eggs, peeled
  and chopped (optional—
  serve on the side)

Remove as much meat from the turtle bones as possible and season the meat with the Seafood Seasoning Mix. In a heavy saucepan, heat the oil over medium heat and fry the turtle meat until it is nicely browned on all sides. While the meat is browning, put the turtle bones into a large stockpot with the 3 quarts of water, the 2 carrots, the ¼ bunch of parsley, the bay leaf, and the stalk of celery. Bring the water to a boil, then reduce the heat to a rolling simmer.

When the turtle meat is browned, add the flour and make a medium-brown roux, stirring constantly over medium heat. Add the onions, the chopped celery, the minced carrots, bell pepper, and garlic and sauté in the roux mixture for 5 minutes. Add the tomato purée and blend it into the roux well. Add the Beef Stock and cook this mixture for 30 minutes over very low heat, stirring often.

Add the lemon juice, Worcestershire sauce, Tabasco sauce, 3 bay leaves, sweet basil, thyme, black pepper, white pepper, garlic powder, onion powder, and the liquid that the turtle bones have been simmering in. (Be sure to strain the liquid before adding it to the pot.) Reduce the heat to simmer and cook for 15 minutes.

Chop the turtle meat into small pieces and add it to the simmering mixture. Cook at a low simmer for 30 minutes, then add the sherry, salt, and ½ cup of parsley and simmer for 5 minutes. Serve hot in individual serving bowls with chopped egg if desired. Serves 8.

Lagniappe: This dish may be made in advance and either refrigerated or frozen. To reheat, just thaw in the refrigerator if frozen and heat over low heat until hot, adding eggs if desired. This is an excellent appetizer for any meal. About 260 calories per serving without the chopped egg or 280 calories with the chopped egg.

CRAWFISH BISQUE

For the stuffed crawfish heads:

48 large live crawfish or cleaned crawfish heads from the market
water to cover crawfish
2 pounds of fresh peeled crawfish tails and their fat
2 large yellow onions, finely chopped
1 medium bell pepper, finely chopped
1 cup of minced celery
1 tbsp. of minced garlic
1 stick of unsalted butter
2½ cups of diced French bread

milk
1½ tsp. of Seafood Seasoning Mix (see index for recipe)
½ tsp. of Tabasco sauce
1 tbsp. of Worcestershire sauce
½ tsp. of black pepper
½ cup of minced fresh parsley
1 cup of minced green onion tops
½ cup of evaporated milk
1 egg, beaten
flour

For the bisque:

1 cup of peanut oil
¾ cup of all-purpose flour
2 medium onions, chopped
1 small bell pepper, chopped
2 stalks of celery, chopped
2 cloves of garlic, minced
1 15-ounce can of stewed tomatoes
3 tbsp. of tomato paste
1 pound of fresh crawfish tails
½ gallon of crawfish water (from first cooking step), Seafood Stock, or Chicken Stock (see index for recipes)

1 tsp. of Seafood Seasoning Mix (see index)
½ tsp. of salt
¼ tsp. of Tabasco sauce
2 bay leaves
½ tsp. of sweet basil
¼ tsp. of thyme
½ cup of minced green onions
¼ cup of minced fresh parsley
cooked white rice

To make the stuffed crawfish heads:

Soak live crawfish in fresh water for 15 minutes, then clean each one well. Put them in a large stockpot and cover with plenty of fresh cold water (at least 1 gallon). Place pot over medium heat and bring the water to a boil, then reduce heat to simmer and let the crawfish cook for 1 to 3 hours at a low simmer.

Remove the crawfish from the water after cooking, reserving the water for later use. Let the crawfish cool until you can handle them easily. Clean one crawfish at a time as follows: break off and discard the tail; separate the head from the body (just behind the eyes); and use your thumb to clean out the body. This body shell is what you will stuff. Repeat this process until all the crawfish are cleaned. Wash the shells and set them aside.

To make the stuffing:

Grind together the crawfish tails and fat, the chopped large onions, the chopped medium bell pepper, the minced celery, and the tablespoon of minced garlic until well ground. (You can use a food processor and chop everything very fine if a grinder is not available.) In a heavy metal pot over medium heat, sauté this mixture in the butter for 12 minutes, stirring often. While sautéing the vegetables, soak the French bread in enough milk to soften it, then squeeze the milk out of the bread and set the bread aside.

When the sautéing time is up, add the soaked bread, Seafood Seasoning Mix, Tabasco sauce, Worcestershire sauce, black pepper, parsley, green onion, evaporated milk, and egg and remove from the heat. Stir stuffing until completely blended. Stuff 1 to 1½ table-spoons of stuffing into each crawfish body shell. Roll the shells in flour. Place on a baking sheet and bake at 350 degrees for 20 minutes. Remove from oven and let cool.

To make the bisque:

As the shells go into the oven, begin to make the bisque. In a heavy saucepot over medium heat, heat the peanut oil until hot. Add the ¾ cup of flour to make the roux, stirring constantly until the roux is golden brown. Add the chopped medium onions, the small chopped bell pepper, the chopped celery, and the 2 minced garlic cloves and sauté for 5 minutes. Add the tomatoes without their liquid (reserve the liquid) and sauté for 7 minutes, stirring constantly.

Add the tomato liquid, tomato paste, crawfish tails, and crawfish water. Bring to a slow boil, then reduce to a low simmer and add the Seafood Seasoning Mix, salt, Tabasco sauce, bay leaves, sweet basil, and thyme. Simmer for 1 hour over very low heat. Then add the stuffed crawfish shells, the ½ cup of green onion, and the ¼ cup of parsley and simmer for 10 more minutes. Serve hot over cooked white rice. Serves 8. This is real Cajun eating!

Lagniappe: This dish may be (and almost has to be) made in advance and either refrigerated or frozen. If you are going to freeze it, keep the heads separate and freeze them just before baking. The bisque itself can be completely made and frozen. To serve, take the stuffed heads from the freezer and bake them, frozen, for 25 minutes at 350 degrees. Heat the bisque to a low simmer and add the heads, green onion, and parsley to the bisque, then serve hot over the rice.

You can also make this recipe in its various parts and assemble it when ready to serve. This is a real company dish that shows you really care. About 573 calories per serving of this outstanding dish. No reduction or change in this recipe is recommended.

COLE SLAW

1 small head of green
  cabbage, shredded
½ small head of purple
  cabbage, shredded
2 green onions, shredded
2 tbsp. of minced fresh
  parsley
1 clove of garlic, finely
  minced

1 cup of mayonnaise
½ cup of sour cream
½ tsp. of Tabasco sauce
1 tbsp. of lemon juice
1 tsp. of freshly ground black
  pepper
salt to taste

Mix both cabbages, the green onion, parsley, and garlic. Cover tightly and refrigerate for 1 hour. In a separate bowl, mix the mayonnaise, sour cream, Tabasco sauce, lemon juice, and black pepper. Cover dressing tightly and refrigerate for 1 hour. Pour the dressing over the vegetables and toss until the vegetables are well coated. Add salt and toss well. Cover tightly and refrigerate for at least 1 hour. Serve chilled. Serves 8 to 10.

Lagniappe: This salad can be made a day or even 2 days in advance and stored in the refrigerator. Do not freeze. It is excellent with all fried seafood or with a sandwich. About 205 calories per serving in 10 servings or 255 calories per serving in 8 servings.

CRAWFISH SALAD

2½ cups of peeled and diced
   boiled crawfish
½ cup of finely chopped
   celery
¼ cup of minced green
   onion
2 tbsp. of minced bell
   pepper
¼ cup of finely chopped
   sweet pickles

2 hard-boiled eggs, chopped
¼ tsp. of Tabasco sauce
¼ tsp. of Worcestershire
   sauce
¼ tsp. of freshly ground
   black pepper
½ cup of mayonnaise
salt to taste

Combine all of the ingredients except the salt and mix until well blended. Taste and season with salt if needed (the crawfish should be well seasoned from the crawfish boil). Serve warm or chilled. Serves 4.

Lagniappe: This salad is an excellent way to use crawfish left over from a crawfish boil. It can be made up to 2 days in advance but is best when served the day it is made.

You can use this recipe to make **Shrimp Salad** by substituting 2½ cups of peeled, deveined, and diced boiled shrimp for the crawfish. To make **Lump Crabmeat Salad,** use 1 pound of fresh lump crabmeat in place of the crawfish. The crawfish version has about 371 calories per serving; the shrimp version about 398; and the lump crabmeat version about 374.

POTATO SALAD

2½ pounds of red unpeeled
  potatoes
3 extra-large eggs
cold water to boil potatoes
1½ tsp. of salt
¼ cup of finely chopped
  onion
⅓ cup of sweet pickle relish
  or chopped sweet pickles
⅓ cup of finely chopped
  celery

2 tbsp. of diced pimento
2 tsp. of prepared mustard
½ tsp. of black pepper
1 tsp. of salt
¼ tsp. of white pepper
1 tbsp. of minced fresh
  parsley
¼ cup of very finely chopped
  green onion tops
1 cup of mayonnaise

Wash the potatoes and put them in a large pot. Add the eggs in their shells and fill the pot with cold water to just above the potatoes and eggs. Add the salt and place over high heat. Boil at a rolling boil until the potatoes are tender when pierced with a table fork. Remove the potatoes and eggs from the boiling water and let them cool until they are cool enough to handle.

Use a knife and remove the skin from the potatoes, then chop them into large dice and put them into a large bowl. Peel the eggs, chop them well, and add them to the potatoes. Add the onions, pickle relish, celery, pimento, mustard, black pepper, salt, white pepper, parsley, and green onion tops. Toss lightly until well mixed. Add the mayonnaise and mix well. Serve immediately, or refrigerate and serve chilled. Serves 8.

Lagniappe: Do not freeze. You can make this up to 2 days ahead and refrigerate it, but be careful not to leave it out of the refrigerator for too long or it will spoil. I like potato salad best just after it is made, when it is still slightly warm. This is excellent with many dishes and a real treat with gumbo. About 341 calories per serving.

CAJUN FRENCH SALAD DRESSING

½ cup of vinegar
½ tsp. of Tabasco sauce
1 tbsp. of dark brown sugar
1 tbsp. of light brown sugar
2 tbsp. of chili sauce
2 tbsp. of catsup
¼ small onion, finely
   minced
2 cloves of garlic, finely
   minced

1 tsp. of salt
1 tsp. of sweet basil
1 tsp. of paprika
¼ tsp. of onion powder
¼ tsp. of garlic powder
1 tsp. of fresh lemon juice
¼ tsp. of dry hot mustard
¼ tsp. of filé powder
1 egg white
2 cups of salad oil

Place the vinegar, Tabasco sauce, sugars, chili sauce, catsup, onion, and garlic in a food processor. Blend at high speed until the sugars are dissolved. Add the salt, sweet basil, paprika, onion powder, garlic powder, lemon juice, mustard, filé powder, and egg white. Blend at high speed for 1 minute.

With the processor running on low power, slowly drizzle the oil through the opening at the top into the processor until all the oil has been poured in. Refrigerate until ready to use. Serve on any green salad; it is also excellent on avocados. Makes about 3 cups of dressing.

Lagniappe: This is a great make-ahead salad dressing that will keep in your refrigerator for about 1 week. If you do not have a food processor, a blender will do. Or, you can mix by hand with a wire whisk, but be prepared to have a sore arm. About 85 calories per tablespoon or 28 calories per teaspoon of dressing.

QUICK POPPY SEED DRESSING

¼ medium yellow onion, as
   fresh as possible (you
   want it juicy)
2 cups of sugar
2 tsp. of white pepper
2 tsp. of dry hot mustard

¼ tsp. of Tabasco sauce
1 tbsp. of lemon juice
¾ cup of white vinegar
2 cups of quality salad oil
¼ cup of poppy seeds

This is a food processor dressing. Place the onion in the processor, turn it on full power, and let it run until the onion liquifies. Add the sugar, white pepper, mustard, Tabasco sauce, lemon juice, and vinegar. Turn the processor on full power and blend for 1 minute. The sugar should dissolve in the vinegar.

With the processor running on low speed, drizzle the salad oil into the center of the processor until all of the oil is blended in. Mix in the poppy seeds in the same manner, mixing for 30 seconds more after the poppy seeds are blended in. Pour into a quart jar and store in the refrigerator to use as needed. If the mixture starts to separate, just shake the jar rapidly a few times to remix the ingredients. Makes about 1 quart of dressing. Excellent over fruit or any salad greens.

Lagniappe: Talk about a wonderful dressing! It keeps for a couple of weeks in the refrigerator and is so much better in quality than the poppy seed dressings you buy at the store. It is so easy to make that you can always keep plenty on hand.

If you do not have a food processor, you can use a blender, but it may take a little more time, and it may be harder to chop up the onion. You can add the vinegar to the onion to make it easier to chop. If you are really eager, you can make this dressing by hand using a good wire whisk; just beat it until you turn blue. About 85 calories per tablespoon or 28 calories per teaspoon of dressing.

RED WINE SALAD DRESSING

⅓ cup of hearty burgundy wine
⅓ cup of vinegar
⅓ cup of sugar
⅓ cup of fresh lemon juice
2 cloves of garlic, finely minced
1 tbsp. of very finely minced fresh parsley

1 tsp. of minced bell pepper
1 tbsp. of Worcestershire sauce
½ tsp. of Tabasco sauce
1 bay leaf
1 tsp. of dry mustard
½ tsp. of salt
⅔ cup of quality olive oil

Place the wine, vinegar, sugar, lemon juice, garlic, parsley, bell pepper, Worcestershire sauce, and Tabasco sauce into a large bowl and beat well with a wire whisk until the sugar is dissolved. Add the bay leaf, mustard, and salt, then slowly beat in the olive oil. Let the dressing stand at room temperature for 4 hours, then refrigerate. Makes a little over 2 cups of dressing.

Lagniappe: It is very easy to make this dressing in a food processor or blender. Just put in all the ingredients except the olive oil and mix on high speed for 1 minute. Slowly drizzle in the olive oil until well mixed. Let stand as above. Excellent on top of any green salad. It keeps in the refrigerator for about a week. About 48 calories per tablespoon of dressing or about 16 per teaspoon.

Seafood

What a great bounty the state of Louisiana has been blessed with! Our shores offer such an abundant supply of mouth-watering seafood that it is hard to understand why seafood is not a part of our daily menus. Not only is seafood a great food, but it is also low in calories compared to main-dish meats. Even at today's prices, seafood is a good buy because the cost per serving is reduced by the variety of inexpensive ingredients that can be added. A pound of crabmeat goes a long way. Although it can cost as much as $9.25 in the off-season, a pound of crabmeat prepared in a sauce will feed 6 people, so the cost per person is relatively low. The same is true for shrimp, crawfish, and oysters, but the initial price is never as high as for lump crabmeat.

Perhaps the only drawback to seafood is that it doesn't keep for a long period of time. You have to have a fresh product, cook it soon, and serve it right away. We also tend to overcook seafood, reducing it to tasteless mush. Do not overcook! Seafood is such a delicate product that you must treat it with care to enjoy it as it was meant to be enjoyed.

The Acadians were very lucky to have been transplanted from the cold, harsh, bitter land of Canada to the warm bayou country filled with every sort of fresh seafood the mind can imagine. They learned immediately that "les fruits de bayou" were culinary treats not to be ignored. Add spice and variety to your menus; cook with seafood often as a main dish and/or as an appetizer.

HOT CRABMEAT DIP

1 stick of unsalted butter
4 green onions, chopped
¼ cup of chopped celery
¼ cup of chopped bell
  pepper
2 cloves of garlic, minced
1½ tbsp. of flour
½ cup of milk
8 large mushrooms, sliced
8 ounces of cream cheese,
  softened and cut into
  pieces

¼ tsp. of Tabasco sauce
1 tbsp. of Worcestershire
  sauce
½ tsp. of black pepper
¼ tsp. of white pepper
½ tsp. of sweet basil
½ tsp. of onion powder
1 pound of lump crabmeat
crackers or small pastry
  shells

Melt the butter in a medium saucepan over medium heat. Sauté the green onions, celery, bell pepper, and garlic for 6 minutes. Add the flour and cook for 3 minutes, stirring constantly. Add the milk and blend until well mixed. Add the mushrooms and coat them with the sauce. Add the cream cheese, reduce the heat to low, and cook, stirring constantly, until the cream cheese is melted.

Add the Tabasco sauce, Worcestershire sauce, black pepper, white pepper, sweet basil, and onion powder and blend well. Lightly fold in the crabmeat. Place dip in a chafing dish or over a warmer. Keep warm, but do not let the dip burn over too high a heat. Serve with crackers or small pastry shells. An excellent appetizer. Serves 10 to 15.

Lagniappe: You can make this dip up to a day in advance and refrigerate it. Be careful not to stir it too much when you heat it up or you will break up the large lumps of crabmeat. Do not freeze this dip. Ten servings have about 232 calories each; 15 servings, about 155. To this, add about 12 calories for each saltine cracker, about 22 for each unsalted cracker, or about 36 for each pastry shell.

CRABMEAT ÉTOUFFÉE

1 stick of unsalted butter
1 large onion, chopped
1 medium sweet red pepper,
  diced
2 tbsp. of minced celery
1 clove of garlic, minced
1 pound of fresh lump
  crabmeat
1 tbsp. of flour
1 cup of water
½ tsp. of Tabasco sauce

¼ tsp. of white pepper
¼ tsp. of freshly ground
  black pepper
1 tsp. of salt
1 tsp. of paprika
¼ cup of minced fresh
  parsley
¾ cup of minced green
  onion
cooked white rice

Melt the butter in a large skillet over medium heat. Add the onion, red pepper, celery, and garlic and sauté until the onions are clear and limp (about 5 minutes). Add the fresh crabmeat and sauté for 1 minute. Blend in the flour and cook for 2 minutes, stirring constantly. Add the water and blend well. The sauce should thicken and become smooth.

Add the Tabasco sauce, white pepper, black pepper, salt, and paprika; blend in well. Reduce the heat to low simmer and cook for 15 minutes. Add the parsley and green onion and cook for 3 minutes. Serve at once over cooked white rice. Serves 4 to 6.

Lagniappe: This recipe may be made in advance and stored in the refrigerator until you are ready to use it. Do not add the parsley and green onions until you are ready to heat and serve. To heat the étouffée, simmer it over low heat for about 3 minutes, then add the parsley and green onion and heat for 2 minutes. Serve at once. The recipe may also be frozen without the parsley and green onion; you do lose some of the quality by freezing, but the taste is still excellent. When ready to use, thaw in the refrigerator, then follow the same procedure for heating from the refrigerator.

If you are hand-picking the crabmeat yourself, you can mix white lump and claw meat. The dish won't be as pretty, but the flavor will be excellent. Four servings have around 348 calories each without rice and 460 calories each with ½ cup of cooked rice. Six servings have only about 232 calories each without rice and 344 calories each with rice.

LUMP CRABMEAT DES GLAISES

½ cup of mayonnaise
¼ cup of finely minced onion
⅛ cup of finely minced fresh parsley
¼ tsp. of Tabasco sauce
½ tsp. of Worcestershire sauce
1 tsp. of Dijon-style mustard

1 tsp. of dry white wine
½ tsp. of salt
1 pound of lump crabmeat
¼ cup of seasoned bread crumbs
2 tbsp. of grated Parmesan cheese
2 tbsp. of grated Romano cheese

Preheat oven broiler. In a mixing bowl, combine the mayonnaise, onion, parsley, Tabasco sauce, Worcestershire sauce, mustard, wine, and salt. When this is well blended, fold in the crabmeat gently. In another mixing bowl, combine the bread crumbs and cheeses. Divide the crabmeat evenly into 6 individual serving dishes (ceramic shells, ramekins, or au gratin dishes). Sprinkle the bread crumb mixture equally over each dish.

Place in the oven and broil for about 5 minutes or until the mixture bubbles and the bread crumbs are golden brown. Serve hot. Serves 6.

Lagniappe: You can make this recipe in advance and refrigerate it before broiling. Simply cover the dishes with foil or plastic wrap. This dish does not freeze well. As another option, you can serve it family-style in one large baking dish (the new large au gratin dishes would be nice). Delicious—and only around 246 calories per serving.

CRABMEAT AU GRATIN

1 large onion, minced
½ cup of minced celery
1 clove of garlic, minced
¼ cup of minced bell pepper
1 stick of butter
½ cup of all-purpose flour
1 13-ounce can of evaporated
  milk
¼ cup of heavy cream
3 large egg yolks, beaten
1 tsp. of salt
¼ tsp. of Tabasco sauce
¼ tsp. of white pepper
½ tsp. of black pepper

1 pound of lump white
  crabmeat
½ cup of grated Swiss
  cheese
2 tbsp. of diced pimento
1 tbsp. of diced fresh
  parsley
2 tbsp. of finely chopped
  green onion tops
½ pound of grated sharp
  cheddar cheese
butter to grease baking
  dish(es)

Preheat the oven to 375 degrees. In a large saucepan over moderate heat, sauté the onion, celery, garlic, and bell pepper in the butter until the vegetables are wilted (about 5 minutes). Blend the flour in well until all the liquid is absorbed. Remove from the heat, add the evaporated milk, and blend well.

In a mixing bowl, combine the whipping cream and egg yolks and add some of the vegetable-liquid mixture to it. Pour this into the saucepan and return to the heat. Add the salt, Tabasco sauce, white pepper, and black pepper. Cook over low heat for 5 minutes or until the sauce is well blended and thick. Carefully add the crabmeat, Swiss cheese, pimento, parsley, and green onion and blend well, taking care not to tear the lumps of crabmeat.

Pour into lightly greased individual au gratin dishes or into a shallow 2-quart casserole. Cover with the grated cheddar cheese. Bake at 375 degrees for 15 minutes or until the casserole is golden brown. Serve hot. Serves 6.

Lagniappe: You may make this dish in advance and refrigerate it before baking for up to 3 days. You can also freeze it either before or after baking. To freeze it after baking, be sure to cover tightly. To reheat, thaw in the refrigerator until defrosted, then bake at 300 degrees for 12 to 15 minutes. To freeze before baking, just thaw in the refrigerator, then follow the directions above for baking.

You can also use this recipe to make **Crawfish au Gratin;** just substitute 1½ pounds of crawfish for the pound of crabmeat and proceed as above. The crabmeat version has about 450 calories per serving, and the crawfish version has about 461 calories per serving.

CAJUN BOILED CRABS

4 gallons of water
4 pounds of unpeeled medium red potatoes
4 unpeeled white onions
4 unpeeled yellow onions, sliced
2 cayenne peppers, cut into thirds
3 lemons, sliced
3 bay leaves
1 bunch of parsley, washed

4 stalks of celery
5 unpeeled cloves of garlic, crushed
5 whole cloves
5 whole allspice
20 black peppercorns
1¼ 26-ounce boxes of salt
6½ dozen live crabs, cleaned with tap water
8 ears of fresh corn, cleaned

Place the water, potatoes, onions, cayenne peppers, and lemons in a very large stock or gumbo pot (about 10 gallons). Bring the water to a boil over high heat. Boil at a rolling boil for 10 minutes, then add the bay leaves, parsley, celery, garlic, cloves, allspice, peppercorns, and salt. Boil for 5 minutes.

Add the crabs and bring the water back to a boil, then boil for 15 minutes. After 5 minutes, add the corn and continue to boil for 10 more minutes. Remove the crabs, potatoes, and corn. Serve after allowing the crabs to cool slightly for about 3 minutes. You may chill the crabs before serving if you like, but they are great right from the pot. Serves 6 to 8.

Lagniappe: This is a complete dinner meal; you can serve a green salad with it if you like. I don't suggest you do any of this in advance, except perhaps get your seasonings lined up and ready for the pot.

For crabs only, there are about 400 calories in each of 6 servings and about 300 in each of 8 servings. Each ear of corn will add about 70 calories to the calorie count, and each potato will add about 104 calories. If 8 people each eat a potato, an ear of corn, and ⅛ of the crabs, the total calorie count for this very filling meal is only about 474 calories per person. If you want to add a few more calories, use either the **Cajun Cocktail Sauce** or the **Hot Dipping Sauce for Seafood** (see index for the recipes) to really add zest to your meal.

CRABMEAT CYPREMORT

¼ cup of unsalted butter
1 pound of lump crabmeat
1 tbsp. of flour
1 cup of half-and-half
¼ cup of sherry
3 egg yolks, well beaten

¼ cup of heavy cream
½ tsp. of salt
¼ tsp. of Tabasco sauce
¼ tsp. of onion powder
⅛ tsp. of white pepper

Preheat the oven to 300 degrees. Melt the butter in a heavy skillet over medium heat. Sauté the crabmeat in the butter for 3 minutes. Add the flour, blend well, and sauté for 1 more minute. Add the half-and-half and sherry. Reduce the heat to low and simmer for 5 minutes, stirring enough to keep the mixture from sticking to the skillet.

In a small mixing bowl, combine the egg yolks and heavy cream. When the simmering time is up, add about ¼ cup of the hot mixture to the egg mixture. Blend well, then pour the contents of small bowl into the skillet. Stir well. Add the salt, Tabasco sauce, onion powder, and white pepper and mix well. Spoon the crab mixture into 6 individual ceramic shells, ramekins, or au gratin dishes and bake at 300 degrees for 20 minutes. Serve at once. Serves 6.

Lagniappe: This dish may be completely made and placed in the serving dishes, then refrigerated until you are ready to bake and serve; just follow the directions above. You can also freeze this dish, but the quality and texture of the crabmeat will diminish. If you do freeze it, let the dishes defrost in the refrigerator. When you are ready to bake, stir each serving dish to mix in any liquid that may have separated, then bake at 300 degrees for 20 minutes. Only about 340 calories per serving; both delicious and low in calories!

FRIED CRAWFISH TAILS

peanut oil for deep-frying
1 pound of fresh crawfish
  tails, cleaned
2 tsp. of Seafood Seasoning
  Mix (see index for recipe)

2 large eggs, beaten
1 cup of milk
1½ cups of flour

Preheat the oil to 375 degrees in a deep-fat fryer. Season the crawfish tails with 1 teaspoon of the Seafood Seasoning Mix and set them aside. Mix the eggs and milk in one bowl and the flour and the remaining teaspoon of Seafood Seasoning Mix in another bowl. Dip several crawfish at once into the egg mixture, then coat them well with the flour mixture. Drop the battered crawfish into the hot fryer and cook until they are golden brown, about 5 minutes. Drain on paper towels and serve at once. Serves 4.

Lagniappe: Do nothing in advance. The crawfish tails are only great when they are just fried, so don't try to serve them as leftovers; it's not worth it. However, they do make excellent sandwiches! Place some hot crawfish in a bun or between 2 slices of bread with mayonnaise and a little Creole mustard. Add lettuce, tomato, and a couple of pickle slices and you've got a great **Crawfish Sandwich.** About 400 calories per serving (without bread).

JAMBALAYA AUX ECREVISSES
(CRAWFISH JAMBALAYA)

1 strip of bacon, chopped
2 tbsp. of unsalted butter
1 large onion, chopped
2 cloves of garlic, minced
¼ cup of minced celery
¼ cup of finely chopped
   bell pepper
2 large tomatoes, skinned
   and chopped
½ tsp. of chili powder
¼ tsp. of white pepper
¼ tsp. of black pepper
¼ tsp. of cayenne pepper

¼ tsp. of Tabasco sauce
2 cups of Chicken Stock (see
   index for recipe) or
   chicken broth
1 pound of crawfish tails
1½ tsp. of salt
1 cup of uncooked long-grain
   rice
½ cup of finely chopped
   green onion
¼ cup of minced fresh
   parsley

In a large saucepan over medium heat, fry the bacon until it is brown and crisp. Melt the butter in the saucepan, then add the onion, garlic, celery, and bell pepper and sauté for 5 minutes. Add the tomatoes and brown them for 3 minutes, then add the chili powder, white pepper, black pepper, cayenne pepper, and Tabasco sauce and mix well.

Add the Chicken Stock, crawfish tails, salt, and rice. Mix very well, then cover and heat until the dish begins to boil. Lower the heat to a slow simmer and cook, covered, for 20 minutes. Reduce the heat to a very low warm and let the dish stand for 15 minutes, covered. Then add the green onion and parsley and mix well. Cover and let the jambalaya stand for 5 more minutes on very low heat. Serve hot. Serves 6.

Lagniappe: You can make this dish in advance and store it in the refrigerator for up to 3 days. You can also freeze this dish without much loss of texture or quality. To serve, just thaw it in the refrigerator and heat it over very low heat until it is warm. Be sure to stir the dish often to prevent sticking. You can also place it in a baking dish and heat it, covered, at 325 degrees for about 15 minutes.

To make **Jambalaya aux Crevettes (Shrimp Jambalaya),** just substitute 1 pound of peeled and deveined shrimp for the crawfish. You can also make **Jambalaya aux Crabes (Crab Jambalaya)** by substituting 1 pound of lump crabmeat or claw meat for the crawfish. This is real heavenly eating for only about 265 calories per serving.

CRAWFISH DALY

2 10-ounce packages of frozen broccoli

boiling water to cover broccoli

1 stick of unsalted butter

1 medium onion, minced

1 small bell pepper, finely chopped

2 stalks of celery, finely chopped

3 cloves of garlic, minced

1 bunch of green onions, chopped (keep tops and bottoms separate)

2 pounds of fresh crawfish tails

1 10¾-ounce can of cream of mushroom soup

1 10¾-ounce can of cream of chicken soup

1 12-ounce jar of Cheez Whiz

1 10-ounce can Ro-tel stewed tomatoes

3 cups of cooked white rice

½ cup of minced fresh parsley

1½ tsp. of salt

½ tsp. of black pepper

¼ tsp. of white pepper

1 tbsp. of Worcestershire sauce

¼ tsp. of Tabasco sauce

½ tsp. of onion powder

¼ tsp. of garlic powder

¼ tsp. of ground bay leaves

¼ tsp. of filé powder

½ tsp. of sweet basil

Place the frozen broccoli in a shallow saucepan. Cover it with boiling water and set aside. In a large saucepan, melt the butter over medium heat. Add the onion, bell pepper, celery, and garlic and sauté for 3 minutes, stirring often. Add the green onion bottoms and sauté for 3 minutes, stirring often. Add the crawfish tails and sauté for 5 minutes, stirring constantly. Add the 2 soups, Cheez Whiz, Ro-tel, and rice. Mix until the Cheez Whiz is melted.

Drain the broccoli and add it to the crawfish mixture with all the remaining ingredients. Blend very well, making sure that the spices are evenly distributed throughout. Pour into a shallow 3- to 3½-quart casserole dish. Bake at 325 degrees for 40 to 45 minutes or until the top is lightly browned and the sides are bubbling. Serve hot. Serves 10 to 12.

Lagniappe: This is quick and easy Cajun cooking from cans that makes an excellent one-dish meal. The blending of these flavors and the ease of preparation make this an excellent quick dish. You can mix it in advance and store it for up to 24 hours in the refrigerator. You can also freeze this dish without hurting the quality and texture too much; just prepare and bake as directed, then cover tightly and freeze. To serve, thaw in the refrigerator until defrosted and bake at 300 degrees until hot, about 12 to 15 minutes. Ten servings have about 253 calories each, and 12 servings have about 211 calories each.

CRAWFISH SKILLET MARIE LOUISE

¼ cup of peanut oil
1 stick of unsalted butter
1 pound of fresh crawfish tails
1 tablespoon of minced celery
1 tablespoon of very finely minced carrots
1 bunch of green onions, chopped
2 medium bell peppers, sliced into strips
2 firm red tomatoes, sliced into wedges

8 large fresh mushrooms, sliced
2½ cups of cooked white rice
1¼ tsp. of salt
½ tsp. of Tabasco sauce
½ tsp. of freshly ground black pepper
¼ tsp. of sweet basil
¼ tsp. of filé powder
1 tbsp. of dry white wine
¼ cup of toasted sliced almonds
½ cup of finely minced fresh parsley

In a very heavy large skillet, heat the peanut oil over medium-high heat until it begins to smoke. Add the butter and move it around so that it melts quickly. Add the crawfish tails, celery, and carrots and sauté for 3 minutes. Add the green onions and mix well. Add the bell peppers, mix well, and sauté for 30 seconds. Add the tomatoes, mix well, and sauté for 30 seconds. Add the mushrooms and stir just until juices coat each mushroom slice.

Add the rice, salt, Tabasco sauce, black pepper, sweet basil, filé powder, and wine and mix until all of the rice is coated with the pan liquid. Add the almonds and parsley and mix very well. Serve at once. Serves 8.

Lagniappe: Do not freeze or refrigerate this dish. The texture and quality of the vegetables will deteriorate if not served at once. Besides, the dish does not take long to cook (less than 10 minutes), so there is no need to make it in advance. I do suggest that you chop all of the ingredients up and arrange them in order to speed up your cooking time. This is a great one-dish meal. Serve it with French bread and a fruit salad with poppy seed dressing.

You can substitute shrimp for the crawfish and make **Shrimp Skillet;** just use about 1¼ pounds of fresh peeled and deveined medium shrimp instead of crawfish and cook as above, sautéing for 4½ minutes instead of 3 minutes after adding the shrimp. Each serving has only about 295 calories. Easy, tasty, and low in calories, this recipe is a real winner!

CRAWFISH THOMAS

2 strips of bacon, chopped
½ stick of butter
2 cloves of garlic, minced
¼ cup of flour
2 cups of milk
¼ cup of freshly squeezed
   lemon juice
8 ounces of sliced
   mushrooms
4 green onions, chopped
½ cup of brandy
½ pound of peeled and
   deveined boiled shrimp,
   chopped
2 pounds of crawfish tails

1½ cups of grated Swiss
   cheese
1 cup of sharp cheddar
   cheese
½ tsp. of Tabasco sauce
1½ tsp. of salt
½ tsp. of black pepper
½ tsp. of white pepper
¼ tsp. of red pepper
¼ tsp. of sweet basil
¼ tsp. of celery seed
½ cup of finely chopped
   fresh parsley
½ cup of dry bread crumbs

In a large saucepan, fry the bacon pieces over medium heat until they are crisp and brown. Add the butter and heat until melted. Place the garlic in the pan and sauté for 2 minutes. Add the flour and blend well. Reduce the heat to medium-low and cook for 4 minutes, stirring constantly. Remove from the heat and add the milk. Stir with a heavy wire whisk until the flour is dissolved in the liquid. Add the lemon juice and mix well. Add the mushrooms and green onions and cook over medium-low heat, stirring often, until the sauce thickens, about 5 to 7 minutes.

Add the brandy and shrimp and mix until the brandy is absorbed. Add the crawfish, cheeses, Tabasco sauce, salt, black pepper, white pepper, red pepper, sweet basil, celery seed and parsley and blend well. Place in a shallow 3-quart casserole dish or 10 individual au gratin dishes. Top with the bread crumbs. Bake for 40 minutes at 350 degrees, then remove from the oven and let stand for 3 minutes before serving. Serve hot. Serves 10.

Lagniappe: You can make this dish up to the baking part and store for up to 2 days in the refrigerator before baking as above. I do not recommend freezing this dish, as it tends to become quite grainy. After it is baked, you can also refrigerate it for up to 2 days. To reheat, just bake at 350 degrees for about 12 minutes. This is a very rich and filling main dish. You can substitute crabmeat for the crawfish to make **Crabmeat Thomas.** I would suggest using lump crabmeat or king crabmeat so you won't have to pick out a lot of shells. About 395 calories per serving.

CRAWFISH NICOLE

1½ tbsp. of bacon fat
2 sticks of unsalted butter
1 large onion, chopped
¾ cup of chopped bell pepper
2 cloves of garlic, minced
½ cup of chopped celery
½ pound of fresh mushrooms, sliced
1½ pounds of peeled crawfish tails
⅓ cup of flour
1 13-ounce can of evaporated milk
1 cup of milk
¼ cup of cream sherry

¼ cup of freshly squeezed lemon juice
1 cup of sour cream
1¼ tbsp. of Dijon-style mustard
1 tsp. of dry hot mustard
½ tsp. of Tabasco sauce
½ tsp. of black pepper
¼ tsp. of white pepper
1½ tsp. of salt
½ cup of finely chopped green onion
½ cup of minced fresh parsley
½ cup of dry bread crumbs

In a large heavy saucepan, melt the bacon fat and 1 stick of butter over medium heat. Sauté the onion, bell pepper, garlic, and celery for 5 minutes. Add the mushrooms and sauté for 3 minutes. Add the crawfish tails and sauté for 4 minutes. Remove the crawfish and vegetables from the pan, leaving as much of the liquid as possible. Set the crawfish and vegetables aside in a bowl for later use.

Add the other stick of butter to the saucepan and melt over medium heat. Add the flour and cook, stirring constantly, for 3 minutes. Remove from the heat and stir in the evaporated milk, milk, cream sherry, lemon juice, and sour cream. Whip well with a wire whisk. Return the sauce to low heat. Add the Dijon-style mustard, dry hot mustard, Tabasco sauce, black pepper, white pepper, and salt. Cook the sauce for 5 minutes, stirring constantly. Add the green onion and parsley and cook for 1 minute. Add the crawfish and vegetables from the bowl and blend well.

Pour the mixture into individual au gratin dishes or one large baking dish and top with bread crumbs. Bake at 400 degrees for 10 to 12 minutes or until the top is golden brown. Let stand for 5 minutes before eating. Serve hot. Serves 8 to 10.

Lagniappe: You can make this dish in advance and store it in the refrigerator for up to 48 hours; refrigerate before putting it into the baking dish or au gratin dishes to bake. Do *not* freeze this dish! The sauce will break apart.

This recipe also allows a great deal of flexibility. Use 1½ pounds of lobster meat cut into bite-size pieces instead of the crawfish and you have **Lobster Nicole.** The only other change necessary will be to cook the lobster for 5 minutes instead of 4 minutes as for crawfish. Use 1½ pounds of peeled and deveined shrimp in place of the crawfish and make **Shrimp Nicole.** You will need to cook the shrimp for 6 minutes instead of 4. Use 1 pound of lump crabmeat instead of the crawfish and make **Lump Crabmeat Nicole.** Cook the crabmeat for only 1 minute. To make **Scallops Nicole,** use 1½ pounds of fresh bay scallops instead of the crawfish. Cook them for 5 minutes. Don't let this be all the varieties you try; the list is endless. Here is the calorie information for each serving:

	In 8 servings	In 10 servings
Crawfish Nicole	460	368
Lobster Nicole	479	383
Shrimp Nicole	475	380
Lump Crabmeat Nicole	451	360
Scallops Nicole	468	374

CRAWFISH CASSEROLE CANTRELLE

1 stick of unsalted butter
1 cup of chopped onion
1 cup of finely chopped celery
1 cup of chopped bell pepper
1 10-¾ ounce can of cream of mushroom soup
1 cup of Seafood Stock (see index for recipe)
1 cup of chopped green onion
½ cup of chopped parsley
¼ cup of diced pimento

1 pound of peeled crawfish tails
2½ cups of cooked white rice
1 cup of grated Velveeta cheese
1½ tsp. of salt
½ tsp. of black pepper
½ tsp. of Tabasco sauce
¼ tsp. of white pepper
¼ tsp. of garlic powder
butter to lightly grease casserole dish
½ cup of dry bread crumbs

In a large skillet, melt the butter over medium heat. Sauté the onion, celery, and bell pepper until the onion is clear and limp, about 5 to 7 minutes. Add the soup and stir it in. Add the Seafood Stock, green onion, parsley, pimento, and crawfish tails. Reduce the heat to low and let the dish simmer for 5 minutes.

Add the rice, Velveeta, salt, black pepper, Tabasco sauce, white pepper, and garlic powder. Blend well, then pour into a lightly greased 2½- to 3-quart casserole dish. Sprinkle evenly with the bread crumbs. Bake at 375 degrees for 30 to 40 minutes or until the top is golden brown and the sides are bubbling. Serve hot. Serves 6.

Lagniappe: This dish may be made completely in advance, then placed in the refrigerator to bake as much as 12 hours later. When you are ready to bake, just follow the directions above. To freeze this dish, bake it as above, then let it cool, cover it tightly, and freeze. To reheat, just let it thaw in the refrigerator and bake at 325 degrees for 15 minutes.

As another serving suggestion, this dish looks nice and serves nicely in individual dishes such as au gratin dishes or ceramic shells. You can also freeze in these dishes for a quick individual meal from the freezer. About 391 calories per serving.

CRAWFISH STEW

½ cup of cooking oil
½ cup of flour
2 medium onions, chopped
1 bell pepper, chopped
2 stalks of celery, chopped
2 cloves of garlic, minced
2 pounds of peeled crawfish
   tails (with fat if it is fresh)
1 tsp. of salt
½ tsp. of Tabasco sauce

½ tsp. of freshly ground
   black pepper
1 cup of water
½ cup of chopped green
   onion
¼ cup of chopped fresh
   parsley
1 tbsp. of fresh lemon juice
cooked white rice

Make a roux with the cooking oil and flour over medium heat in a heavy saucepan. Stir the flour until it is golden brown; do not let it stick. When brown, add the onions, bell pepper, celery, and garlic and sauté in the roux for 4 minutes. Add the crawfish tails, salt, Tabasco sauce, and black pepper. Cook for 2 minutes. Add the water and simmer over low heat, covered, for about 10 minutes, stirring once or twice during the cooking time.

Uncover and add the green onion, parsley, and lemon juice. Cook for 5 to 10 minutes until the stew comes to the consistency you like. (There will be a difference in the stew's consistency every time you make it. This is because of the crawfish; some have more liquid than others, but you can adjust that during the final simmering.) Serve hot over cooked white rice. Serves 8.

Lagniappe: This dish may be made in advance and cooked up to the adding of the green onion, parsley, and lemon juice. It can then be refrigerated or frozen. When ready to serve, thaw and follow the recipe from the addition of the green onion on. You will find that this dish will improve in flavor when served on the second day. Count on about 260 calories without rice, and about 372 calories per serving with ½ cup of cooked white rice.

CRAWFISH ÉTOUFFÉE

1 stick of unsalted butter
1 large onion, chopped
¼ cup of finely chopped
celery
¼ cup of chopped bell
pepper
2 cloves of garlic, minced
1 pound of peeled fresh
crawfish tails
1 tsp. of salt
½ tsp. of black pepper

¼ tsp. of white pepper
½ tsp. of Tabasco sauce
½ tsp. of onion powder
1½ tbsp. of flour
½ to 1 cup of Seafood Stock
(see index for recipe) or
water
½ cup of minced green onion
¼ cup of minced fresh
parsley
cooked white rice

In a large skillet over medium heat, melt the butter. Add the onions, celery, bell pepper, and garlic and sauté until the onions are limp and clear, about 5 minutes. Add the crawfish tails and season with the salt, black pepper, white pepper, Tabasco sauce, and onion powder. Blend well and cook over medium heat for 5 minutes. Add the flour and blend well, stirring constantly to prevent the flour from burning.

When the flour is blended in and has cooked for about 2 minutes, add the Seafood Stock slowly. Blend in the stock well, lower the heat to simmer, and let the dish cook for 20 minutes, stirring now and then to prevent sticking. About 3 minutes before the end of the cooking time, add the green onion and parsley. Stir in well and cook for the remaining 3 minutes. Serve hot over cooked white rice. Serves 6.

Lagniappe: There is no doubt that this dish is best when the crawfish are just cooked, but it does refrigerate well for up to 2 days and can be frozen with excellent results. Completely finish the cooking process before you freeze or refrigerate the dish (put it in a container that closes tightly). To reheat, thaw in the refrigerator if frozen and heat at a low simmer until hot. Serve over the cooked white rice. About 220 calories per serving without rice or about 332 calories per serving with ½ cup of rice.

BROILED OYSTERS CHARLAND

36 large fresh oysters, shucked
12 strips of bacon, cut into thirds
1½ tsp. of Seafood Seasoning Mix (see index for recipe)

2 tbsp. of lemon juice
½ tsp. of Tabasco sauce
2 tsp. of Worcestershire sauce
1 tbsp. of dry white wine

Wrap each oyster with ⅓ of a strip of bacon and fasten the bacon with a toothpick. Sprinkle the oysters with the Seafood Seasoning Mix and place them in a deep mixing bowl. In a small mixing bowl, combine the lemon juice, Tabasco sauce, Worcestershire sauce, and wine and blend well. Pour this liquid over the oysters and marinate for 2 hours, turning the oysters carefully two or three times.

When the 2 hours are up, preheat the oven broiler. When the oven reaches broiling temperature, place the oysters on a cookie sheet covered with aluminum foil. Spoon a little of the sauce on top of each oyster. Broil about 5 minutes or until the bacon is done and the oysters are puffy and begin to curl. Serve hot. Serves 6.

Lagniappe: You can make this appetizer well in advance. It calls for a 2-hour marinating time, but you can marinate it for longer, even up to 24 hours. (Keep it tightly covered.) Broil as directed when ready to serve. Hot French bread is a nice complement. If the oysters are small, double the number you would normally serve and use a smaller piece of bacon to wrap each. About 466 calories per serving. No way to cut down on calories here except to skip the dish, but you will be missing out on a treat!

FRIED OYSTERS

2 tsp. of Seafood Seasoning
  Mix (see index for recipe)
½ cup of flour
¼ tsp. of baking soda
¼ tsp. of baking powder
1 tsp. of cornstarch
2 dozen fresh large oysters

2 large eggs, beaten
¼ tsp. of Tabasco sauce
½ tsp. of Worcestershire
  sauce
1 cup of plain dry bread
  crumbs
cooking oil for deep-frying

Mix the first teaspoon of Seafood Seasoning Mix, the flour, baking soda, baking powder, and cornstarch in a shallow bowl until well blended. Dredge the oysters in the flour mixture one at a time and place them on a plate. Combine the eggs, Tabasco sauce, and Worcestershire sauce in another bowl. Combine the bread crumbs and the other teaspoon of Seafood Seasoning Mix in another bowl. Dip the oysters one at a time into the egg mixture, then roll them in the bread crumbs and seasoning mix. Deep-fry the oysters in 375-degree oil until they are golden brown. Drain on paper towels and serve hot. Serves 2 to 3.

Lagniappe: No way to make this in advance. Fried oysters must be eaten right after they are cooked. About 600 calories per serving if you eat 12 oysters; about 400 if you eat 8. Serve with **Seafood Cocktail Sauce** or **Hot Dipping Sauce for Seafood** (see index for recipes). You can also use this recipe to make **Fried Shrimp;** just substitute shrimp for the oysters.

OYSTERS ROCKEFELLER

4 dozen large oysters,
  shucked (reserve 1 cup of
  liquor and deeper halves
  of shells)
1½ tbsp. of anise seeds
2 cups of water
10 pounds of rock salt
1 bunch of green onions
1 bunch of fresh parsley
1½ pounds of fresh spinach,
  cleaned and trimmed
½ pound of collard greens,
  washed and trimmed
3 stalks of celery, cleaned
½ lead of lettuce, washed
1 bell pepper, cleaned,
  seeds removed
½ pound of endive leaves,
  washed and trimmed
½ pound of mustard greens,
  washed and trimmed

5 strips of bacon, chopped
3 sticks of unsalted butter
1 tbsp. of thyme
4 cloves of garlic, finely
  minced
¾ cup of flour
3 cups of milk
½ cup of fresh lemon juice
1 tsp. of Tabasco sauce
2½ tsp. of salt
½ tsp. of freshly ground
  black pepper
½ tsp. of white pepper
¼ tsp. of cayenne pepper
½ tsp. of filé powder
¼ tsp. of ground bay leaves
1½ to 3 cups of dry bread
  crumbs
1 cup of Herbsaint liqueur
  or Pernod

Drain the liquor from the oysters well by placing the oysters in a fine strainer and letting the liquor drip into a container. Reserve the liquor for later use. Wash the oyster shell halves well in soap and water, using a hard brush to scrub them if necessary. Dry the shells well with paper towels and set them aside.

In a small saucepan, combine the anise seeds and water. Place over medium heat and bring to a boil. When the water starts to boil, reduce the heat to a low simmer and cover the pot. Allow the anise seeds to simmer until you are ready for them. Pour equal amounts of the rock salt into 8 pie pans and place 6 clean, dry oyster shells on the rock salt in each pan. Set the pans aside.

Using a food grinder or food processor, chop the green onions, parsley, spinach, collard greens, celery, lettuce, bell pepper, endive, and mustard greens. Make sure the greens are chopped very fine.

Set them aside for later use. Fry the bacon in a large saucepan over medium heat until crisp and brown. Add the butter and allow it to melt. Add the thyme and garlic and sauté for 3 minutes. Add the flour and cook over medium-low heat for 5 minutes, stirring constantly to prevent sticking. Add the chopped greens and blend well, making sure the roux is dissolved and blended into the vegetables. Add the milk and oyster liquor and stir well.

Strain the anise seeds from the simmering liquid and add this liquid to the Rockefeller sauce. Blend in well, then add the lemon juice, Tabasco sauce, salt, black pepper, white pepper, cayenne pepper, filé powder, and ground bay leaves. Blend until well mixed. Reduce heat to low and let the sauce cook for 20 minutes, stirring often to prevent sticking.

Place the pie pans in a 425-degree oven for 15 minutes. Remove the oysters from the strainer and pat them dry with paper towels. Remove the pans from the oven after 15 minutes and place one oyster on each shell. When the sauce is cooked, add the dry bread crumbs to it a little at a time until the sauce is thick enough to stay on top of the oysters without running over the sides. Add the Herbsaint liqueur to the sauce and mix well. (Do not skip this part of the recipe, or your Rockefeller will be flat.) Cover each oyster with plenty of sauce.

Return the pie pans to the oven and bake at 425 degrees for 10 to 12 minutes or until the edges bubble and the top starts to brown lightly. Remove from the oven and place each pie pan on a dinner plate. Serve hot. Serves 8.

Lagniappe: The Rockefeller sauce may be made in advance and refrigerated in a tightly covered container for up to 3 days. It is possible to freeze the sauce, but freezing breaks down the consistency somewhat. If you must freeze it (I really don't recommend this, however), defrost it completely in the refrigerator. Place it in a saucepan over low heat, add a small amount of milk, and whip the sauce back into a smooth texture. If you refrigerate, just cover the oysters with the chilled sauce and bake as directed.

The sauce can be used as is over other seafood as well, such as crabmeat to make **Crabmeat Rockefeller,** shrimp to make

Shrimp Rockefeller, or scallops to make **Scallops Rockefeller.** A serving size of 6 oysters will have about 921 calories; a serving of only 3 oysters (appetizer-size) will have about 461 calories.

To reduce the calorie count to 665 calories per serving of 6 oysters, cut out 2 sticks of butter, 2 strips of bacon, and ¼ cup of flour. This will still have the Rockefeller taste and a nice texture, but the richness will be significantly reduced. Three oysters will have about 333 calories in this reduced-calorie version.

OYSTERS BIENVILLE

6 strips of bacon, chopped fine
1 stick of unsalted butter
3 cloves of garlic, minced
1 bunch of green onions, chopped
1 pound of mushrooms, chopped large
⅔ cup of flour
1 quart of hot milk
⅔ cup of oyster liquor
½ cup of sherry
⅓ cup of fresh lemon juice
1 tsp. of Tabasco sauce

⅔ pound of boiled shrimp, peeled and coarsely chopped
¼ cup of minced fresh parsley
¼ cup of minced green onion tops
1 tsp. of salt
¼ tsp. of white pepper
¼ tsp. of black pepper
4 dozen large oysters
4 dozen deep oyster shells, scrubbed clean and dried

Place the bacon in a large saucepan and fry over medium heat until crisp and brown. Add the butter. When the butter is melted, add the garlic, the chopped green onions, and the mushrooms and sauté for about 3 minutes. Add the flour and blend in. Reduce the heat to low and cook the flour for about 5 minutes, taking care not to let it stick or brown.

Add the hot milk a little at a time until the sauce is smooth. Add the oyster liquor, sherry, lemon juice, and Tabasco sauce. Blend in until the Bienville sauce is smooth again. (You may have to use a wire whisk; the sauce sometimes needs to be whipped into a smooth consistency.) Add the shrimp, parsley, minced green onion tops, salt, white pepper, and black pepper and blend into the sauce. Cook over low heat for about 15 minutes. The sauce should thicken nicely.

Set the oven on broil. Place each of the oysters on a shell and broil them for 1½ to 2 minutes. The oysters should curl around the edges and become puffy. Remove the oysters from the oven. Using a spatula, place 2 to 3 tablespoons of the sauce over and around each oyster, completely covering the oyster and filling in all gaps between oyster and shell. Reduce the oven heat to 450 degrees and bake the oysters about 10 minutes or until the tops are lightly browned and the edges are bubbling. Serve immediately. Serves 12 as an appetizer or 6 as a main dish.

Lagniappe: This is the Oysters Bienville recipe I served at Le Champignon Restaurant, including the sauce that so many customers asked me for. You can do so much with it that you will wonder if there's anything it *can't* be used on! You can make it in advance and store it in the refrigerator for as long as 4 days; just keep the container tightly closed. To prepare the dish, use a spatula to place the sauce on top of the oysters and bake as directed.

You can also spoon the sauce over crabmeat in a crab shell to make **Crabmeat Bienville** or over shrimp in a ramekin to make **Shrimp Bienville.** (This is my father's favorite. I even used to serve it to him in an oyster shell. No one ever knew he was eating shrimp while they were eating oysters—until now!)

A serving of 12 oysters has about 1100 calories per serving; a serving of 6 oysters has about 550 calories; and a serving of 3 oysters has about 275 calories. (You can figure around 92 calories per oyster.) No calorie reduction is recommended.

OYSTERS SIDONIA

4 dozen large oysters
16 strips of bacon, cut into thirds
½ cup of burgundy wine
1 tsp. of Tabasco sauce
1 tbsp. of Worcestershire sauce

1 tbsp. of fresh lemon juice
2 cloves of garlic, finely minced
1 tsp. of onion powder
2 tsp. of Seafood Seasoning Mix (see index for recipe)

Wrap each oyster with ⅓ of a strip of bacon and fasten the bacon with a toothpick. Mix the wine, Tabasco sauce, Worcestershire sauce, lemon juice, garlic, and onion powder in a deep bowl until well blended. Add the bacon-wrapped oysters. Let the oysters marinate for 3 hours in the refrigerator.

Remove from the marinade and sprinkle the Seafood Seasoning Mix over all. Bake at 475 degrees for 5 minutes, then baste well with the marinade, turn the oysters over, and bake for 5 more minutes. Baste once more, reduce the heat to 350 degrees, and bake for 5 more minutes. Serve hot. Serves 4 as a main course or 8 as an appetizer.

Lagniappe: You can marinate the oysters for up to 36 hours before baking. Do not cook in advance and refrigerate or freeze; serve the oysters right from the oven. About 954 calories in a dozen wrapped oysters; that makes about 80 calories per oyster. So count out the oysters you want and then multiply by 80 to get the correct calorie count.

OYSTERS OMAR

½ carrot
3 cloves of garlic, peeled
5 large mushrooms, washed
1 stalk of celery, washed
3 green onions, washed,
  roots removed
1 tbsp. of olive oil
½ bunch of parsley, washed
2 medium endive leaves,
  washed and torn into a
  few pieces
3 sticks of butter, softened
¾ tsp. of Tabasco sauce
1¼ tsp. of salt
1 tsp. of freshly ground
  black pepper

¼ tsp. of filé powder
1 tbsp. of Worcestershire
  sauce
½ tsp. of sweet basil
½ tsp. of dry hot mustard
¼ tsp. of ginger
1¼ cup of dry French bread
  crumbs
1 tbsp. of fresh lemon juice
¼ cup of dry sherry
4 dozen oysters, parboiled
  lightly until they puff up
  and curl slightly on the
  edges

Preheat the oven to 500 degrees. In a food processor, chop the carrot, garlic, mushrooms, celery, and green onions at high speed until fine, about 1 to 1½ minutes. Heat the oil in a heavy saucepan over medium heat until hot. Sauté the chopped vegetables over medium heat for 5 minutes, stirring constantly. Place the parsley and endive in the food processor and chop at high speed until the parsley is very fine, about 2 minutes. Make sure that no stems or leaves are left unchopped.

Add the sautéed vegetables to the food processor and blend at high speed for 30 seconds. Add the butter, Tabasco sauce, salt, black pepper, filé powder, Worcestershire sauce, sweet basil, dry mustard and ginger and blend at high speed until the sauce is smooth. Add the bread crumbs, lemon juice, and sherry and blend until well mixed.

Put 4 parboiled oysters into each of 12 small (6-ounce) ceramic soufflé dishes and cover oysters generously with the sauce Omar. Bake at 500 degrees for 5 to 7 minutes or until the tops are brown and bubbly. Serve immediately. Serves 12.

Lagniappe: Do not freeze. You can make the sauce in advance and refrigerate it for up to 3 days. When you are ready to use it, let the sauce soften at room temperature, then whip it lightly with a fork before spreading it on top of the oysters.

You can also use this sauce with 2 pounds of fresh lump crabmeat to make **Crabmeat Omar.** Just put ⅙ of a pound of crabmeat in each of 12 soufflé dishes and cover with the sauce then bake as above. It's wonderful! About 385 calories per serving of the oysters version and about 350 calories per serving of the crabmeat version.

SHERRY SHRIMP

2 pounds of shrimp, peeled and deveined	½ cup of sherry
	½ tsp. of Tabasco sauce
2 tsp. of Seafood Seasoning Mix (see index for recipe)	1 tsp. of Worcestershire sauce
1 stick of unsalted butter, melted	¼ cup of finely minced fresh parsley

Preheat the oven to 400 degrees. Season the shrimp well with the Seafood Seasoning Mix and place them in a shallow baking dish. Mix well the butter, sherry, Tabasco sauce, and Worcestershire sauce and pour over the shrimp. Sprinkle the shrimp with the fresh parsley. Bake at 400 degrees for 20 minutes. Serve hot. Serves 12 as an appetizer.

Lagniappe: This is such an easy dish that there is no reason to do anything in advance except peel and devein the shrimp. You can also season the shrimp in advance and place them in the baking dish if you like. Do not freeze. Serve with toothpicks as an appetizer or in individual serving dishes as a main dish. Only about 126 calories per serving. A wonderful dish; full of flavor, but low in calories.

SHRIMP BONIN

1 pound of large shrimp
1 tsp. of Seafood Seasoning
   Mix (see index for recipe)
1 medium onion, sliced and
   separated into rings

1 stick of unsalted butter
1 tbsp. of olive oil
½ cup of brandy

Peel and devein the shrimp, leaving the tip of the tail on each. Butterfly the shrimp by splitting each one along the back almost completely through and spreading the halves apart into a butterfly shape. Season the shrimp evenly with the Seafood Seasoning Mix. Combine the shrimp and onion rings well in a mixing bowl. Cover the bowl tightly with plastic wrap and let it refrigerate for at least 2 hours.

In a large, heavy skillet over medium heat, melt the butter, then add the olive oil. When the butter starts to turn light brown, add the shrimp and onions. Sauté for 5 minutes, shaking the pan gently to keep the shrimp and onions from sticking. Reduce the heat to low and carefully add the brandy. Strike a match away from the pan then tilt the pan a little and light the brandy. Be careful at this stage; there will be a "puff" as the brandy lights. Let the dish burn until it burns itself out. Serve at once. Serves 4 as a main dish or 8 as an appetizer.

Lagniappe: All you can do in advance on this dish is peel and devein the shrimp, cut the onions, and set them aside in the refrigerator. You can let them sit for up to 12 hours if you wish. This will save you some time when you are ready to prepare the dish. This is a quick and showy dish that is excellent for company. About 387 calories per serving as a main dish and about 194 calories per serving as an appetizer.

SHRIMP LEBLANC

2 sticks of unsalted butter
¼ cup of chopped bell
  peppers
¼ cup of chopped onion
3 cloves of garlic, minced
2 tbsp. of minced green
  onion tops
1 tbsp. of finely minced
  celery
2 tbsp. of lemon juice
2 tbsp. of Worcestershire
  sauce

½ tsp. of Tabasco sauce
2 pounds of large shrimp,
  peeled and deveined
½ cup of dry white wine
1 tbsp. of dried parsley
  flakes
1 tsp. of freshly ground black
  pepper
1½ tsp. of salt
½ tsp. of Italian seasoning
½ tsp. of Accent

Melt the butter in a large saucepan over medium heat. Preheat the oven to 375 degrees. In the saucepan with the butter, sauté the bell pepper, onion, garlic, green onion, and celery over medium heat until limp, about 5 minutes. Arrange the shrimp in 8 individual baking dishes and spoon equal amounts of the butter sauce over them.

Combine the remaining ingredients in another saucepan over medium heat. Bring the wine mixture to a boil, then reduce the heat to low and simmer for 5 minutes. Meanwhile, place the baking dishes in the oven and bake at 375 degrees for 10 minutes. Remove the dishes from the oven and spoon equal amounts of the wine sauce into each dish. Stir the wine through and place the dishes back in the oven for another 7 minutes. The shrimp should be a nice pink color. Serve hot with plenty of French bread to soak up the sauce. Serves 8.

Lagniappe: This dish cannot be made in advance. However, you can always prepare all the ingredients in advance and just mix them together as directed. An excellent dish that makes a nice company meal, especially for guests who really like shrimp. This recipe has less than 300 calories per serving, so no change is needed.

BAKED SHRIMP CASSEROLE

2½ pounds of shrimp in
their shells, but heads
removed
1 tbsp. of salt
1 lemon, sliced into circles
1 onion, coarsely chopped
1 bell pepper, chopped
1 stalk of celery
1 tsp. of Tabasco sauce
water to cover shrimp
2½ cups of diced French
bread
½ cup of dry white wine
¼ cup of butter
1 cup of chopped green
onion

¼ cup of finely chopped bell
pepper
1 clove of garlic, minced
¼ cup of minced celery
4 hard-boiled eggs, chopped
1 cup of cooked white rice
1 cup of evaporated milk
¼ tsp. of Tabasco sauce
½ tsp. of salt
¼ tsp. of dry mustard
⅛ tsp. of nutmeg
¼ cup of finely chopped
fresh parsley
butter to grease casserole
dish

Preheat the oven to 350 degrees. Place in a large saucepan the shrimp, salt, lemon, onion, chopped bell pepper, celery stalk, and the teaspoon of Tabasco sauce. Add water to cover ingredients and bring to a hard boil over high heat. Allow the shrimp to boil for 3 minutes, then remove from heat and drain. Cover the shrimp with fresh cold water to stop the cooking process.

Peel and devein the shrimp, then separate the shrimp into two equal piles. Chop one of the piles; leave the other shrimp whole. In a large mixing bowl, soak the French bread in the wine. Wash the large saucepan that you used to boil the shrimp and melt the butter in it over medium heat. Sauté the green onion, the ¼ cup of chopped bell pepper, the garlic, and the minced celery until limp, about 3 to 4 minutes. Add the shrimp and wine-soaked bread and cook over low heat for 2 minutes.

Remove from heat and add the remaining ingredients. Mix well and pour into a greased 3-quart casserole dish. Bake at 350 degrees for 30 minutes. Serve hot. Serves 6 to 8.

Lagniappe: This dish may be made in advance and refrigerated or frozen. Thaw in the refrigerator (if frozen) before baking as directed. You can also serve this dish in individual casseroles or au gratin dishes, which are great to have on hand in the freezer. About 467 calories in each of 6 servings and about 350 calories in each of 8 servings. No calorie reduction recommended (or even needed).

SHRIMP ÉTOUFFÉE

1 stick of unsalted butter
3 medium onions, chopped
½ cup of very thinly sliced celery
2 cloves of garlic, minced
3 tbsp. of diced bell pepper
1 tbsp. of tomato paste
2 pounds of shrimp, peeled and deveined
2 tbsp. of flour
1 tsp. of salt

1½ tsp. of Seafood Seasoning Mix (see index for recipe)
½ tsp. of Tabasco sauce
½ cup of Seafood Stock (see index for recipe) or water
1 cup of chopped green onion
¼ cup of minced parsley
cooked white rice

In a large, heavy skillet, melt the butter over medium heat. Sauté the onions, celery, garlic, and bell pepper until the onions are lightly browned around the edges, about 7 minutes. Add the tomato paste and blend well. Add the shrimp and cook over medium heat until they are nicely pink through and through, about 5 minutes. Add the flour and blend well. Add the salt, Seafood Seasoning Mix, and Tabasco sauce. Stir well and cook 1 minute.

Add the Seafood Stock and lower the heat. Blend well. Cover the skillet and let the dish simmer for 12 to 15 minutes, stirring often to prevent sticking. Remove the cover, add the green onion and parsley, and cook for 3 minutes. Serve at once over cooked white rice. Serves 8.

Lagniappe: This dish lends itself to being made ahead of time. You can either refrigerate or freeze the dish after it has been completely cooked. To reheat, just thaw in the refrigerator and heat over medium-low heat until the shrimp are hot, then serve over rice.

If you want to have a frozen meal ready to heat in the microwave, just place a ½-cup serving of cooked white rice in the center of an au gratin dish and spoon one-eighth of the shrimp and sauce around the rice. Cover the dish with a good plastic wrap, taking care to seal all edges (I like to tape down the sides with freezer tape), and freeze. When you are ready to serve, take the dish from the freezer and punch 2 small holes in the top of the plastic wrap. Set the dish in the center of the microwave. Heat it on high power for 5 minutes or until hot. A really nice dish for only about 210 calories without rice and 322 calories with ½ cup of cooked white rice. Low in calories but great in taste!

SHRIMP ÉTIENNE

36 jumbo shrimp
1½ tsp. of Seafood
  Seasoning Mix (see index
  for recipe)
2 sticks of unsalted butter,
  melted

½ tsp. of Tabasco sauce
1 tsp. of Worcestershire
  sauce
3 large fresh lemons, cut in
  half

Pell and devein the shrimp, leaving the tip of the tail on each. Split each shrimp along the back almost completely through. Season shrimp with the Seafood Seasoning Mix. Place 6 shrimp in each of 6 au gratin dishes or ceramic shells. Combine the melted butter, Tabasco sauce, and Worcestershire sauce and pour over the shrimp, putting equal amounts in each dish (use all of the butter mixture).

Bake dishes at 450 degrees for about 8 minutes. Remove dishes and set the oven on broil setting. Place dishes under the broiler (about 6 inches away from the heat) for 5 minutes. The shrimp should take on a nice golden-brown color on the edges and a beautiful pinkish-orange in their centers. Remove from the oven and squeeze half a lemon over each of the 6 serving dishes. Serve at once. Serves 6.

Lagniappe: This is such a simple dish that there is no reason to make it in advance. In fact, you can't; it needs to be served right away for peak freshness. You can, however, peel and season the shrimp and set them aside in the refrigerator until you are ready to bake them. Under 350 calories per serving!

SHRIMP CREOLE

½ cup of cooking oil
2 large onions, coarsely chopped
1 large bell pepper, coarsely chopped
1 cup of chopped celery
2 cloves of garlic, minced
2½ cups of whole peeled tomatoes, chopped
1 tsp. of salt
1 tbsp. of paprika
½ tsp. of Tabasco sauce

¼ tsp. of black pepper
¼ tsp. of finely ground filé powder
1 tsp. of sweet basil
¼ tsp. of thyme
1 large bay leaf
3 pounds of shrimp, peeled and deveined
2 tbsp. of cornstarch
a little cold water
cooked white rice

Heat the oil in a large saucepan over medium heat until hot. Add the onions, bell pepper, celery, and garlic. Sauté until all the vegetables are limp and the onions are clear, about 5 minutes. Add the tomatoes and continue to sauté until the tomatoes are lightly browned, about 5 minutes. Add the salt, paprika, Tabasco sauce, black pepper, filé, sweet basil, thyme, and bay leaf. Lower the heat and simmer for 15 minutes. Add the shrimp and simmer for 12 minutes.

To thicken the mixture, dissolve the cornstarch in as little cold water as it takes to dissolve it. Add this to the saucepan; the sauce should thicken quickly. Serve at once over cooked white rice. Serves 6 to 8.

Lagniappe: This dish freezes and takes refrigeration well. Do not add the cornstarch before you refrigerate or freeze it; freeze after the shrimp are added. To heat, thaw in the refrigerator if frozen and heat in a saucepan to simmering, then add the cornstarch as directed above. If you are cooking to refrigerate, stop the process after cooking for about 9 minutes once the shrimp have been added. Cool, then refrigerate. Heat as directed for freezing.

This is the Creole that was served at Le Champignon Restaurant (another secret given away!). Six servings have around 356 calories without rice and about 468 with ½ cup of cooked white rice. In 8 servings, figure about 267 calories per serving without rice or about 379 calories with rice. Already low in calories; no reduction needed.

STUFFED SHRIMP

24 jumbo shrimp
3 tbsp. of bacon fat
1 stalk of celery, finely chopped
½ medium bell pepper, finely chopped
1 large onion, finely chopped
2 cloves of garlic, minced
1 pound of lump crabmeat
¼ cup of finely chopped green onion
¼ cup of minced fresh parsley
2½ tbsp. of flour
2 large eggs, well beaten
¼ tsp. of Tabasco sauce
1 tsp. of salt

¼ tsp. of black pepper
¼ tsp. of paprika
¼ tsp. of onion powder
⅛ tsp. of ground bay leaves
½ cup of flour
1 tbsp. of Seafood Seasoning Mix (see index for recipe)
2 eggs, well beaten
1 tsp. of water
¼ tsp. of Tabasco sauce
1½ cups of French bread crumbs
1 tsp. of Seafood Seasoning Mix (see index)
2½ cups of cooking oil

Peel and devein the shrimp, leaving the tip of the tail on each. In a large, heavy skillet, melt the bacon fat over medium heat. Add the celery, bell pepper, onion, and garlic and sauté for 4 minutes. Add the crabmeat, green onion, and parsley, lower the heat to medium-low, and sauté for 4 minutes. Add the 2½ tablespoons of flour and blend it in. Remove from the heat and mix in the 2 large eggs, the ¼ teaspoon of Tabasco sauce, salt, black pepper, paprika, onion powder, and bay leaves. Blend well.

Place the shrimp on a flat surface and cut the tail open, but not all the way through. Mix the ½ cup of flour and the tablespoon of Seafood Seasoning Mix. Coat each shrimp with the flour mixture. Spoon about 1 tablespoon of the crabmeat stuffing onto each shrimp and mold it to the tail. Mix the 2 eggs, the water, and the other ¼ teaspoon of Tabasco sauce. Mix the bread crumbs and the teaspoon of Seafood Seasoning Mix.

Dip the stuffed shrimp one at a time into the egg mixture, then coat well with the bread crumb mixture. Place on a sheet of waxed paper on a large cookie sheet. When all the shrimp are coated, cover them with waxed paper and refrigerate for at least 1 hour. When you are ready to fry the shrimp, heat the oil to medium-high in a skillet and fry the shrimp 4 at a time until they are golden brown. Drain on a paper towel. Serve hot. Serves 4 to 6.

Lagniappe: As noted, this recipe must be made in advance up to the frying step. The shrimp fry better after being chilled. You can place them in a 200-degree oven after frying to keep them warm if you like so they will remain uniform in temperature. This is an excellent company dish. You can do all the preparation in advance and only have to fry the shrimp right before you are ready to serve them. Do not try to reheat the already-fried shrimp; they lose their character and flavor rapidly after cooking. Each stuffed shrimp has about 133 calories. Count on about 800 calories per serving in 4 servings or about 533 calories in 6 servings.

BEER-BATTER SHRIMP

2 pounds of shrimp	1 tbsp. of cooking oil
2 egg whites	1 tsp. of garlic salt
⅔ cup of beer	salt and pepper to taste
1 cup of all-purpose flour	flour to coat shrimp
1½ tbsp. of baking powder	cooking oil for deep frying

Peel and devein the shrimp, leaving only the tip of the tail on each. Mix the egg whites, beer, flour, baking powder, the tablespoon of oil, garlic salt, and salt and pepper. Add the shrimp to the batter and let them sit in the batter for 2 hours in the refrigerator. When ready to cook, roll the shrimp in flour and deep-fry them at 375 degrees until the shrimp are golden brown and float to the top. Serve at once. Serves 6.

Lagniappe: All you can do in advance is make the batter, put the shrimp in it, and refrigerate. You can do this up to 12 hours in advance. Serve right after frying for best results. Do *not* freeze. This dish has fewer than 300 calories per serving. A real treat!

This recipe is from my mother-in-law, Rose LeBlanc, of Lake Charles, Louisiana.

CAJUN BOILED SHRIMP

1 gallon of cold tap water
⅓ cup of salt
2 large unpeeled onions, washed and cut into fourths
2 cayenne peppers or 1 jalapeño pepper
3 stalks of celery, cut into 2-inch pieces
2 lemons, sliced into circles
¼ bunch of parsley with stems
10 black peppercorns

1 small bell pepper, cut into fourths
3 bay leaves
½ tsp. of sweet basil
3 whole cloves
2 unpeeled cloves of garlic, crushed
3 whole allspice
2 tbsp. of sugar
2 tbsp. of Worcestershire sauce
4½ pounds of unpeeled large shrimp, heads removed
½ tsp. of Tabasco sauce

In a large gumbo or stockpot, place the cold water, salt, and onions. Bring the pot to a hard boil over high heat. Cut one of the cayenne peppers into fifths and place it in the pot with the remaining whole cayenne pepper. (If you are using a jalapeño, just cut it in half.) Add the celery, lemons, parsley, peppercorns, bell pepper, bay leaves, and sweet basil. Once the water is at a hard boil again, reduce the heat and let the pot stay at a slow boil for 15 minutes.

Add the cloves, garlic, allspice, sugar, and Worcestershire sauce. Return the heat to high and add the shrimp. When the water begins to boil again, add the Tabasco sauce and boil for exactly 3 minutes, then remove the pot from the heat and scoop the shrimp out of the water. Serve hot right from the pot or chill and serve later. Serves 6.

Lagniappe: You can boil shrimp in advance and refrigerate them for up to 24 hours without any loss of quality. After cooking, keep the liquid and allow it to cool completely, then store the shrimp in this liquid in the refrigerator to keep them at their best. When you are ready to serve, either remove the shrimp from the liquid and serve them chilled or return the pot to the heat and let it simmer over low heat until the shrimp are warmed, about 5 minutes after the liquid begins to simmer slowly.

You can freeze boiled shrimp after peeling, but their texture and quality will be significantly reduced. It is much better to boil the shrimp as you need them. There are only about 220 calories per serving of boiled shrimp, so it is really a nice low-calorie meal.

ALMOND SHRIMP

1 pound of shrimp
½ cup of butter
1 cup of slivered almonds
1 cup of chopped green
  onion
¾ tsp. of salt
½ tsp. of Tabasco sauce

¼ tsp. of black pepper
1 tbsp. of finely minced fresh
  parsley
1 tsp. of Worcestershire
  sauce
1 tbsp. of dry white wine

Peel and devein the shrimp, leaving the tip of the tail on each. Melt the butter over medium heat in a large skillet. Sauté the almonds and green onion for 4 to 5 minutes or until the almonds are lightly browned. Remove the almonds and green onion from the skillet, being careful to leave as much butter as possible. Add the shrimp and sauté for 4 minutes or until they are a nice pink color all over.

Add the salt, Tabasco sauce, black pepper, parsley, Worcestershire sauce, and wine. Lower the heat and simmer for 3 minutes so the flavors blend. Add the almonds and green onion and mix well. Sauté for 1 minute just to heat the almonds and green onion. Serve hot. Serves 4.

Lagniappe: This is an excellent company dish. You can prepare the dish up to adding the seasonings, then remove from heat and refrigerate, keeping the almonds and green onion separate from the shrimp. When ready to serve, return the seasoned shrimp to the skillet and sauté for 2 minutes, then add the almonds and green onion and sauté them with the shrimp for 2 more minutes. Serve at once.

I suggest dishing the servings out into individual ramekins or au gratin dishes so the juices stay with the shrimp and don't run all over your plate. About 663 calories per serving. (Oh, come on—live a little!)

POISSON AU SHERRY

1 pound of fresh fish fillets, cut into serving pieces
butter to grease baking dish
½ cup of finely chopped onion
1 tbsp. of minced celery
½ tsp. of finely minced garlic

8 large mushrooms, neatly sliced
½ cup of cream sherry
1 tbsp. of fresh lemon juice
¼ tsp. of Tabasco sauce
½ tsp. of salt
½ tsp. of freshly ground black pepper
1 tsp. of olive oil

Preheat the oven to 350 degrees. Place the fish fillets in a greased 3-quart baking dish. Cover them with the onion, celery, garlic, and mushrooms. Pour the cream sherry, lemon juice, and Tabasco sauce over the fillets. Sprinkle the salt and black pepper evenly over the fillets, then drizzle the olive oil over them. Bake at 350 degrees, uncovered, for 30 minutes. Serve hot with the sauce from the pan on the side. Serves 4.

Lagniappe: You can put this dish together in advance and store it in the refrigerator until you are ready to bake it. Do not cook the dish before storing it! Fresh fish should be eaten right after it is cooked so the natural flavors remain. A real low-calorie treat for under 200 calories per serving.

BAKED TROUT VERMILION

2 large (3-pound) trout, cleaned but with heads on
½ stick of butter, softened
1 small onion, chopped
¼ bell pepper, cut in strips

1 large clove of garlic, finely minced
8 large mushrooms, neatly sliced
juice of 1 lemon
¼ tsp. of Tabasco sauce

Preheat the oven to 325 degrees. Slit the fish completely in half lengthwise. Rub both fish with the butter, outside and inside; be sure to use all the butter. Combine the onions, bell pepper, and garlic and stuff the inside cavities of the 2 fish with equal amounts of this mixture.

Place the fish in a 3-quart (or larger) baking dish that has a cover and bake at 325 degrees for 45 minutes. Remove the fish from the oven and add the sliced mushrooms. Return to the oven, cover, and cook for 15 more minutes. Mix the lemon juice and Tabasco sauce. When the fish has finished baking, pour this mixture over the fish. Serve at once. Serves 4 to 8.

Lagniappe: Fresh fish is best eaten when it is freshly cooked. You can prepare the fish for baking, then refrigerate it until 1 hour before serving time. Four servings have around 569 calories each; 8 servings have around 285 calories each.

FISH CHER AMI

1 tsp. of Seafood Seasoning
  Mix (see index for recipe)
4 8-ounce fish fillets
butter to grease baking dish
1 large onion, sliced into
  thin circles

1 cup of sour cream
¼ cup of dry white wine
1 tbsp. of flour
1 tsp. of paprika
1 tsp. of lemon juice
¼ tsp. of Tabasco sauce

Preheat the oven to 350 degrees. Season the fish fillets equally with the Seafood Seasoning Mix. Place the fillets in a greased shallow baking dish. Arrange the onion circles on top of the fillets. Mix the remaining ingredients in a small mixing bowl. Pour this mixture over the fillets. Bake for 30 minutes, uncovered, or until the fish is tender. Serve hot. Serves 4.

Lagniappe: So little time is required to prepare this dish that making it ahead would not serve much purpose. If you like, you can do everything except the baking and store the dish in the refrigerator tightly covered with plastic wrap until you are ready to bake. After the dish is cooked, serve it at once. It does not keep well or reheat well. Under 300 calories per serving.

PAN-CRUSTED REDFISH

4 redfish fillets (about 12
  ounces each)
½ stick of unsalted butter,
  melted
¼ tsp. of Tabasco sauce
12 tsp. of Seafood Seasoning
  Mix (see index for the
  recipe)

4 tbsp. of unsalted butter
4 tbsp. of melted unsalted
  butter

Check each redfish fillet to be sure that there are no bones remaining. Combine the ½ stick of melted butter with the Tabasco sauce in a shallow bowl. Dip the fillets into the mixture. Sprinkle 1½ teaspoons of Seafood Seasoning Mix over each side of each redfish fillet and rub the seasoning in with your fingers.

Place a very heavy metal skillet over high heat and allow it to get very hot. Add 1 tablespoon of the unsalted butter to the pan, then add the first seasoned fillet. Let it cook for 2 minutes on one side, then flip it over to the other side and add 1 tablespoon of melted butter to the pan. (This will cause a great deal of smoke, so be sure that the fan in your stove hood works well; better yet, cook the fish outside over a butane burner. It will give you the heat you need but will not smoke up your house. Also, keep in mind that the skillet could catch fire because of the high temperature.) Cook the first fillet for 2 minutes on the second side.

When the fillet is completely cooked, wipe the pan very carefully with a few paper towels to remove the burned butter and seasonings. Put the cooked fish on a warm plate and place it in a 170-degree oven to keep it warm until you are ready to serve it. Repeat the process until all of the fish are cooked. Serve hot. Serves 4.

Lagniappe: This is *not* a make-ahead dish. You have to eat it right after it is cooked. Besides, the cooking time is very short. Be sure to wear something to protect your clothing while cooking; the skillet splatters and smokes a lot.

Less than 520 calories per serving, and the taste is divine. Don't be concerned by the appearance of the fish; it will look burnt, but the flavor will be excellent and there will be no burnt taste. You can use trout fillets instead of redfish to make **Pan-Crusted Trout.** You can also use red snapper fillets and make **Pan-Crusted Red Snapper.** For the trout, cut down the cooking time to about 1½ minutes on the first side and 1 minute on the second. For the red snapper, cook the first side about 2½ minutes and the second side about 2 minutes.

FISH ROLLS FORTIER

4 fish fillets (about 8
  ounces each)
1 tsp. of Seafood Seasoning
  Mix (see index for recipe)
1 tbsp. of bacon fat
2 tbsp. of unsalted butter
1 stalk of celery, minced
½ cup of minced onion
1 clove of garlic, minced
1 tbsp. of finely chopped bell
  pepper
1 cup of French bread
  crumbs

1 egg, well beaten
1 tbsp. of lemon juice
2 tbsp. of white wine
2 tbsp. of water
1 tsp. of Worcestershire
  sauce
4 slices of bacon
melted butter to coat fish
  rolls
¾ cup of half-and-half
butter to grease baking dish

Preheat the oven to 500 degrees. Season the fillets equally with the Seafood Seasoning Mix, making sure to get both sides of the fish. Set fillets aside. In a heavy skillet over medium heat, melt the bacon fat and the 2 tablespoons of butter. Sauté the celery, onion, garlic, and bell pepper for 4 minutes. Add the bread crumbs, egg, lemon juice, wine, water, and Worcestershire sauce and blend well. Mixture should be somewhat sticky; if it isn't, add a little more water.

Divide the mixture into fourths, placing one-fourth of the mixture on each fillet. Roll each fillet up like a jelly roll and fasten it with toothpicks. Wrap a slice of bacon around each roll and fasten it with toothpicks also. Coat the rolls with melted butter and place them on their sides in a greased shallow baking dish. Pour the half-and-half around the rolls. Bake at 500 degrees for 12 to 15 minutes or until the tops of the rolls are golden brown. Turn the rolls over about halfway through the cooking time. Serve hot with the pan liquid as a sauce. Serves 4.

Lagniappe: This is an excellent dish to make in advance. Prepare the fish rolls and then refrigerate them, tightly covered, in the buttered baking dish until you are ready to bake them. When ready to cook, proceed as directed from the melted-butter coating step. Do not freeze this dish. About 610 calories per serving.

FISH LOAF

2 cups of flaked cooked
  fresh fish
1½ cups of bread crumbs
½ tsp. of baking powder
⅔ cup of chopped celery
⅓ cup of chopped onion
1 tbsp. of fresh lemon juice
1 cup of milk

1 tbsp. of minced pimento
1 tbsp. of chopped green
  pepper
1¼ tsp. of Seafood
  Seasoning Mix (see index
  for recipe)
¼ tsp. of Tabasco sauce

Preheat oven to 350 degrees. Mix all of the ingredients and form into a loaf in a lightly oiled loaf pan. Bake at 350 degrees until brown and firm, about 30 minutes. Serve warm, sliced like a meat loaf, with your favorite cream sauce on top if you desire. Serves 6.

Lagniappe: This dish can be made in advance and frozen for later use, but it does lose some of its texture if not baked just after it is prepared. It is really a very simple recipe, so making it just before serving is no problem. You can also mix it in advance and refrigerate it for up to 24 hours before cooking. About 258 calories per serving; a nice low-calorie dish.

This recipe is from Louise Solari of Lake Charles, Louisiana.

REDFISH LOUISIANE

1 5- to 6-pound whole redfish (head on), cleaned and deboned
2 tbsp. of olive oil
1 tsp. of salt
¼ tsp. of red pepper
½ tsp. of black pepper
¼ tsp. of onion powder
⅛ tsp. of sweet basil
1 cup of water
½ cup of dry white wine

3 tomatoes, skinned and sliced
1 large onion, chopped
1 large lemon, sliced into circles
1 small lime, sliced into circles
3 large bay leaves
¼ cup of finely minced fresh parsley

Preheat the oven to 350 degrees. Rub the fish liberally with the olive oil. Combine the salt, red pepper, black pepper, onion powder, and sweet basil together. Rub this seasoning mixture all over the fish. Pour the water and wine into a large shallow baking dish and place the redfish in it. Surround the fish with the tomato slices, onions, lemon slices, and lime slices. Place the bay leaves on the fish and cover it with the parsley.

Bake the fish for 1 hour at 350 degrees, basting the fish about every 7 to 10 minutes. When the fish is cooked, remove it from the baking dish, place it on a warm platter, and keep it warm in the oven (200 degrees). Pour the vegetables and basting sauce into a medium-sized saucepan. Reduce the sauce by half over medium-high heat. Pour the sauce over the fish and serve at once. Serves 6.

Lagniappe: Do not refrigerate or freeze this dish. It needs to be eaten right after it is cooked. If you like, you can prepare the fish to be cooked and refrigerate it for up to 6 hours in advance. This will save preparation time when your guests arrive. Count on about 315 calories per serving of this tasty dish.

FROG LEGS SAUCE PIQUANTE

1 cup of peanut oil
½ cup of flour
4 medium onions, chopped
4 cloves of garlic, minced
1 cup of chopped celery
1 large bell pepper, chopped
1 cayenne pepper, finely
  chopped
3 15-ounce cans of stewed
  tomatoes
1½ cups of Seafood Stock
  or Chicken Stock (see
  index for recipes)
½ tsp. of garlic powder

½ tsp. of onion powder
½ tsp. of freshly ground
  black pepper
¼ tsp. of white pepper
½ tsp. of Tabasco sauce
1 tbsp. of Worcestershire
  sauce
1 tbsp. of fresh lemon juice
2 tbsp. of peanut oil
18 medium frog legs,
  cleaned and skinned
2 tsp. of Seafood Seasoning
  Mix (see index for recipe)
cooked white rice

In a large saucepan over medium heat, heat the cup of peanut oil until it is hot. Add the flour and heat, stirring constantly, until the roux is dark brown. Add the onions, garlic, celery, bell pepper, and cayenne pepper and sauté for 5 minutes over medium heat. Add the solid pieces from the stewed tomatoes, reserving the liquid for later use, and sauté for 5 minutes. Add the stock, garlic powder, onion powder, black pepper, white pepper, Tabasco sauce, tomato liquid, Worcestershire sauce, and lemon juice. Bring to a boil, then reduce the heat to a low simmer and simmer the sauce for 1 hour, stirring frequently during the cooking process.

In a heavy skillet over medium heat, heat the 2 tablespoons of peanut oil until hot. Season the frog legs evenly with the Seafood Seasoning Mix, rubbing the seasoning into the meat with your hands. Fry the frog legs (4 or 5 at a time) until they are a nice golden brown on all sides. Set them aside. When the sauce is cooked, add the browned frog legs and stir them in. Continue to simmer for 3 more hours over low heat. Serve hot over cooked white rice. Serves 6 to 8.

Lagniappe: This is an excellent dish that is very popular in Acadiana. It can be made in advance and stored in the refrigerator; in fact, storage seems to improve the flavor, if that is possible. It can also be frozen without any harm to the quality of the dish. To reheat, just thaw in the refrigerator and heat over low heat until the sauce is hot and the frog legs are heated through.

You can also use this recipe to make **Rabbit Sauce Piquante** by substituting either 1 large or 2 small rabbits for the frog legs. Just follow the directions above, substituting Chicken Seasoning Mix for the Seafood Seasoning Mix and Chicken Stock for the Seafood Stock. The rest of the recipe is the same. You can also make **Squirrel Sauce Piquante** by substituting 6 squirrel for the frog legs, Veal Seasoning Mix for the Seafood Seasoning Mix, and Beef Stock for the Seafood Stock. Be creative with this recipe; use your favorite meat and make your own version of sauce piquante.

Six servings will have about 638 calories per serving without rice or 750 calories per serving with ½ cup of cooked white rice. In 8 servings, count on about 470 calories per serving without rice or 582 calories per serving with rice.

Poultry

CHICKEN SAUCE PIQUANTE

1 stewing hen, about 5 pounds, washed and cut into 10 serving pieces
1½ tsp. of Chicken Seasoning Mix (see index for recipe)
1¼ cup of peanut oil
1 cup of flour
2 cups of coarsely chopped onion
1½ cups of chopped celery
1 cup of coarsely chopped bell pepper
3 cloves of garlic, minced
1 16-ounce can of whole tomatoes
1 10-ounce can of Ro-tel stewed tomatoes

1 cup of chopped green onion bottoms
1½ quarts of Chicken Stock (see index for recipe) or chicken broth
1 tsp. of Tabasco sauce
1 tsp. of salt
½ tsp. of black pepper
½ tsp. of white pepper
1 tsp. of monosodium glutamate
½ tsp. of cayenne pepper
1 cup of chopped green onion tops
½ cup of chopped fresh parsley
cooked white rice

Season each piece of chicken equally with the Chicken Seasoning Mix. Sauté the chicken in the peanut oil in a large, heavy saucepan over medium heat until all the pieces are nicely browned. Place the chicken on a platter for later use.

Add the flour to the pot and heat, stirring constantly, until you make a very dark roux. Add the onions, celery, bell pepper, and garlic and sauté for 5 minutes. Add the whole tomatoes and Ro-tel, but not the juice from the cans; set this aside for later use. Break the tomatoes apart and sauté for 5 minutes. Add the green onion bottoms and sauté for 2 minutes.

Carefully add the Chicken Stock (it may splatter). Add the juice from the whole tomatoes and the Ro-Tel and stir until the sauce is smooth. Add the Tabasco sauce, salt, black pepper, white pepper, monosodium glutamate, and cayenne pepper. Reduce the heat and simmer for 2 hours.

Add the chicken and cook for 2½ to 3 hours or until the sauce is rich and tasty and the chicken is tender. Add the green onion tops and parsley and cook for 3 more minutes. Serve hot over cooked white rice. Serves 10 generously.

Lagniappe: Cajun eating at its best. You can make this completely in advance and either refrigerate or freeze it. The flavor seems to improve when it is allowed to sit in the refrigerator for a day. To reheat, just thaw in the refrigerator if frozen and bring the sauce back up to serving temperature over medium heat. If it starts to boil, reduce the temperature to simmer.

One excellent variation of this recipe that I really like is **Rooster Sauce Piquante.** Simply double the recipe and change the hen to a rooster (10 to 12 pounds). You will need to add 4½ quarts of stock, though, because you will cook the sauce for 5 hours at a low simmer after you add the rooster. This makes a much richer sauce piquante. The rooster is just made for this dish. After this much cooking, you will find the meat quite tasty! Of course you can serve 20 people with the rooster version, or you will have plenty of delicious sauce piquante to freeze for later use.

Piquante means "hot" or "peppery," and to be real it must have quite a bite to it. If you can't take this much pepper, you can adjust the seasonings to your own taste. There are about 808 calories per serving without rice in the basic version of this recipe. With ½ cup of rice, the total will come to about 1,020 calories.

To reduce the calories significantly, substitute 2 2½-pound fryers for the hen. Follow the recipe down to the addition of the chicken. Do not add the chicken until the sauce has simmered for 3 hours, then add the chicken and simmer for 1 hour or until the chicken is tender. Add the green onion and parsley according to directions. This will reduce the calories to about 505 per serving without rice or about 617 with rice. The taste will still be great, but not as rich.

POULET LENAIN

3 tbsp. of olive oil
4 chicken breast halves,
  .deboned
1 tsp. of Chicken Seasoning
  Mix (see index for recipe)
1 medium onion, chopped
1 clove of garlic, minced
1 tbsp. of minced celery
2 tbsp. of minced bell pepper
1 pound of unpeeled yellow
  summer squash, cut into
  circles

2 whole tomatoes, diced
½ cup of Chicken Stock
  (see index for recipe) or
  chicken broth
¼ tsp. of Tabasco sauce
½ tsp. of salt
¼ tsp. of black pepper
¼ tsp. of sweet basil
⅛ tsp. of filé powder

In a large skillet over medium heat, heat the olive oil. Wash the chicken well and pat dry with paper towels. Season the chicken evenly with the Chicken Seasoning Mix. When the oil is hot, sauté the chicken breasts until they are evenly browned on all sides. Add the onions, garlic, celery, and bell pepper and sauté for 4 minutes. Add the squash and sauté for 2 minutes. Add the tomatoes and sauté for 2 minutes. Add the remaining ingredients. Reduce the heat to low and simmer, uncovered, for 25 to 30 minutes or until the chicken is tender. Serve hot. Serves. 4.

Lagniappe: This dish is best eaten when it is first cooked. You can refrigerate or freeze it without harming the taste, but the texture of the squash will diminish. To reheat, just thaw in the refrigerator if frozen and bake at 350 degrees for 12 to 15 minutes or until hot. This is a nice low-calorie delight; only about 240 calories per serving for a nice main dish with vegetables. Even if you serve it over ½ cup of cooked white rice, it only has about 350 calories per serving.

BAKED CHICKEN DESIRÉ

4 chicken breasts,
deboned and skinned
1½ tsp. of Chicken
Seasoning Mix (see index
for recipe)
1 stick of unsalted butter,
cut in half
½ tsp. of garlic powder
1 large onion, chopped
1 large bell pepper, chopped
2 cloves of garlic, minced
2 tbsp. of minced celery

2 tbsp. of minced carrots
8 large fresh mushrooms,
sliced
½ cup of minced fresh
parsley
¼ cup of finely chopped
green onion tops
¼ tsp. of Tabasco sauce
½ tsp. of fresh lemon juice
1 cup of dry red wine
butter to grease baking dish

Preheat the oven to 325 degrees. Wash the chicken breasts well and pat them dry with a paper towel. Cut the breasts in half so that you have 8 equal pieces. Season well with the Chicken Seasoning Mix. Melt ½ stick of butter in a heavy skillet and sauté the chicken pieces until well browned on both sides. While the chicken is browning, sprinkle the garlic powder over it. When done, place it on a plate for later use.

Add the other ½ stick of butter to the skillet. When the butter is melted, sauté the onion, bell pepper, garlic, celery, and carrot over medium heat for 5 to 7 minutes, stirring constantly. Add the mushrooms, parsley, and green onion and sauté for 2 minutes. Add the Tabasco sauce, lemon juice, and wine and bring to a boil. When the mixture begins to boil, remove from the heat.

Arrange the chicken in a lightly greased shallow baking dish and pour the wine mixture over it. Cover the dish and bake for 1½ hours at 325 degrees, then uncover and bake at 400 degrees for 10 minutes. Serve hot. Serves 8.

Lagniappe: This dish may be completely made in advance and stored in the refrigerator or freezer for later use. To reheat, just thaw in the refrigerator if frozen and bake, covered, at 325 degrees for 12 to 15 minutes. Serve hot. About 265 calories per serving.

CHICKEN PARMESAN

4 whole chicken breasts,
deboned and skinned
1 tsp. of Chicken Seasoning
Mix (see index for recipe)

¼ cup of Italian bread
crumbs
1 cup of Parmesan cheese
½ tbsp. of peanut oil

Wash the chicken breasts well and pat them dry with paper towels. Season the chicken well with the Chicken Seasoning Mix, rubbing the mixture in. Combine the bread crums and Parmesan cheese.

Heat a large, heavy skillet over medium heat and lightly grease it with the peanut oil. Fry one side of the chicken breast halves in the skillet for 3 minutes. Pat ¼ of the bread crumb-cheese mixture onto the uncooked side of each piece. Reduce the heat to medium-low, turn the chicken over, and fry for 10 minutes. The cheese mixture will stick to the chicken and be lightly brown and crusty when done. Serve hot. Serves 4.

Lagniappe: This dish may be made in advance and either frozen or refrigerated. To reheat, set in a baking dish and heat in the oven at 300 degrees until the chicken is hot. You can cover this chicken with **Chicken Parmesan Sauce** if you like (see index for recipe). It is delicious either with or without sauce.

About 478 calories per serving. To reduce the calories, simply cut the chicken breasts in half and prepare as above. This will reduce the calorie count to about 239 calories per ½ chicken breast—a serving size that is still quite filling.

CHICKEN STEW

1½ tsp. of salt
¼ tsp. of red pepper
½ tsp. of black pepper
¼ tsp. of white pepper
¼ tsp. of paprika
¼ tsp. of garlic powder
1 4- to 5-pound stewing chicken, cut into serving pieces
½ cup of cooking oil
3 tbsp. of flour
2 medium onions, chopped
1 small bell pepper, chopped
1 stalk of celery, chopped
1 clove of garlic, minced
8 large mushrooms, sliced
3 cups of Chicken Stock (see index for recipe) or chicken broth
½ cup of chopped green onion tops
1 tbsp. of minced fresh parsley
¼ tsp. of Tabasco sauce
cooked long-grain white rice

Mix the salt, red pepper, white pepper, black pepper, paprika, and garlic powder and rub this mixture into the washed and dried chicken pieces, covering all the pieces equally. Pour the cooking oil into a large saucepan. Fry the chicken pieces in the saucepan over medium-high heat until they are browned on all sides. Remove the chicken pieces and drain the oil from them.

Lower the heat to medium. Add the flour to the remaining oil and heat, stirring constantly to keep the roux from burning. When the roux is a dark reddish-brown, add the onions, bell pepper, celery, and garlic. Cook until the onions are limp, about 3 to 4 minutes. Add the mushrooms and sauté them for 1 minute. Add the Chicken Stock and the chicken. Cover and cook over very low heat (just simmering) for 2½ hours or until the chicken is tender. Just before serving, add the green onion tops, parsley, and Tabasco sauce. Serve hot over cooked white rice. Serves 6 to 8.

Lagniappe: This dish may be completely made before you need it and refrigerated until you are ready to use it. It also freezes very well. Thaw in the refrigerator if frozen, then heat over very low heat until it is hot enough to serve.

About 1,044 calories per serving in 6 servings without rice and 1,156 calories with ½ cup of cooked white rice. In 8 servings the calorie count is about 783 per serving without rice or 895 per serving with rice.

To reduce the calorie count, substitute 2 2½-pound fryers for the stewing chicken and cook as directed, except you will only simmer the stew for 1 hour or until the chicken is tender. This will cut the calorie count down to about 540 per serving in 6 servings without rice, 652 per serving with rice. In 8 servings, the calorie count will be about 405 per serving without rice or 517 with rice. The taste will still be excellent, but the gravy won't be nearly as rich.

CHICKEN ÉTOUFFÉE

½ cup of cooking oil (peanut oil works best)
2 tsp. of Chicken Seasoning Mix (see index for recipe)
1 3½-pound fryer, cut into serving pieces

2 medium onions, sliced lengthwise
1 small bell pepper, chopped
2 tbsp. of chopped celery
1 clove of garlic, minced
¼ tsp. of Tabasco sauce

Heat the oil in a large, heavy skillet that has a cover. Wash the chicken pieces and dry them well with paper towels. Coat the pieces evenly with the Chicken Seasoning Mix and fry them until they are brown on all sides. Remove the pieces as they brown. When all the chicken pieces are done, return them to the pot. Cover the pieces with the vegetables and add the Tabasco sauce. Cover the skillet and cook over low heat for about 1 hour or until the chicken is tender. Stir the dish about twice during the hour. Serve hot with cooked white rice if you like. Serves 6.

Lagniappe: This dish can be prepared in advance and either frozen or refrigerated until you are ready to use it. To reheat, let the dish thaw in the refrigerator if frozen, then cook it over low heat for 10 minutes or until the chicken is heated through. About 405 calories per serving without rice; about 517 calories per serving with ½ cup of cooked white rice.

CHICKEN ISIDORE

1 3½-pound fryer, cut into serving pieces
1 tsp. of salt
¼ tsp. of red pepper
¼ tsp. of white pepper
¼ tsp. of black pepper
¼ tsp. of onion powder
¼ tsp. of garlic powder
⅛ tsp. of ground bay leaves
⅛ tsp. of dry hot mustard
⅛ tsp. of sweet basil
¼ cup of flour
2 tbsp. of peanut oil
1 clove of garlic, minced
½ cup of chopped onions
1 tbsp. of finely chopped celery
1 tbsp. of finely chopped bell pepper
6 to 8 large mushrooms, neatly sliced
½ cup of Beef Stock (see index for recipe) or beef broth
1 8-ounce can of tomato sauce
1 14½-ounce can of stewed tomatoes
¼ tsp. of Tabasco sauce
½ tsp. of Worcestershire sauce
cooked white rice or cooked noodles

Wash the chicken pieces and pat them dry with paper towels. Mix the salt, red pepper, white pepper, black pepper, onion powder, garlic powder, bay leaves, dry hot mustard, and sweet basil and combine this mixture with the flour. Dredge the chicken pieces in the seasoned flour.

In a large skillet over medium heat, heat the oil until it is very hot. Fry the chicken 2 or 3 pieces at a time until the pieces are brown on all sides. Remove from the skillet and set aside. Add the garlic, onion, celery, and bell pepper and sauté for 3 minutes. Add the mushrooms and sauté for 2 minutes. Pour in the Beef Stock, tomato sauce, stewed tomatoes, Tabasco sauce, and Worcestershire sauce and cook until well blended, about 2 minutes.

Put the chicken back into the skillet, making sure all pieces are coated with sauce. Cover and simmer over low heat for 45 minutes or until the chicken is very tender. Serve hot over cooked white rice or cooked noodles. Serves 4 to 6.

Lagniappe: This dish may be made in advance. Let it simmer for 30 minutes, then let it cool. Refrigerate or freeze until ready to use. Then you will only need to cook it for 15 more minutes; it will be well heated and completely cooked. Without rice, each of 4 servings has about 487 calories; with ½ cup of cooked white rice, about 598 calories; with ½ cup of cooked egg noodles, about 587 calories. In 6 servings, each serving has about 325 calories without rice; with rice, about 437 calories; with egg noodles, about 425 calories. This is an excellent company dish.

CHICKEN HENRIETTE

1 3- to 4-pound fryer, cut into serving pieces
1 tsp. of Chicken Seasoning Mix (see index for recipe)
¼ cup of olive oil
2½ tbsp. of flour
1 14½-ounce can of stewed tomatoes
½ tsp. of salt
¼ tsp. of Tabasco sauce
1 tbsp. of Worcestershire sauce
¼ tsp. of thyme
2 tbsp. of minced fresh parsley
2 cloves of garlic, finely minced
1 bay leaf
1 cup of chopped green onion
¼ cup of chopped bell pepper
1 tbsp. of minced celery
¾ cup of dry white wine
cooked white rice

Wash the chicken pieces and dry them with paper towels. Season the chicken pieces evenly with the Chicken Seasoning Mix. Heat the olive oil over medium heat in a skillet that has a cover. Fry the chicken in the skillet until the pieces are golden brown and crispy. Remove them and set them aside. Add the flour to the skillet and cook over medium-low heat until it browns, stirring constantly to prevent sticking. When the flour is a rich brown, add the tomatoes, salt, Tabasco sauce, Worcestershire sauce, thyme, parsley, and garlic. Reduce heat to low and simmer for 15 minutes.

Add the bay leaf, green onion, bell pepper, celery, and wine. Cook the sauce for 5 minutes, covered. Add the chicken, making sure the sauce coats all of the chicken pieces. Cover tightly and simmer for 45 minutes or until the chicken is tender. Serve hot over cooked white rice. Serves 6.

Lagniappe: This is a great recipe for the cook who likes to get ready in advance. You can cook this dish completely and either refrigerate or freeze it. When you are ready to serve, thaw it in the refrigerator or microwave if frozen and simmer it over very low heat until the chicken is heated through. Be sure to serve hot. About 340 calories per serving without rice or about 452 calories with ½ cup of cooked white rice.

It is also excellent served over noodles. As a different serving idea, place lightly buttered noodles in an au gratin dish, cover them with some sauce, and place a piece of chicken in the dish. Place a slice of Swiss cheese over the chicken and heat it under the broiler until the cheese melts. Serve at once.

BAKED CHICKEN GAUTEROT

1 3-pound fryer
1 tbsp. of Chicken
   Seasoning Mix (see index
   for recipe)
1 large fresh turnip, washed
   and cut into fourths
12 fresh new potatoes,
   cleaned

2 cups of julienned carrots
1 cup of julienned celery
1 bell pepper, julienned
1 large onion, julienned
½ tsp. of Tabasco sauce
2 tsp. of Worcestershire
   sauce
½ cup of dry white wine

Wash the chicken well and cut off any excess fat. Pat the chicken dry with paper towels. Season it well with the Chicken Seasoning Mix; pat the seasoning in with your hands, taking care to get the inside of the chicken as well. Place the chicken in a baking dish and place the turnip quarters inside the chicken cavity. Place the chicken in the oven and bake at 425 degrees for 45 minutes. Add the potatoes to the dish and bake for 15 minutes.

Remove the dish from the oven and take the chicken out; set it aside on a plate. Add to the baking dish the carrots, celery, bell pepper, and onion. Add the Tabasco sauce, Worcestershire sauce, and wine. Stir the vegetables around in the dish, taking care to coat all of them well.

Return the chicken to the dish and set it on top of the vegetables. Baste the chicken with the drippings until all of the chicken is coated. Return to the oven, lower the heat to 400 degrees, and bake for about 30 more minutes or until the chicken is tender (the legs should move back and forth very freely). Remove the chicken from the dish; stir the vegetables once and spoon them out onto a warm platter. Place the chicken in the center of the platter and serve at once. Serves 6.

Lagniappe: This is an excellent dish if you like simple food that has a nice contrast. You have not only your meat, but also a nice array of fresh vegetables. This is not a dish that you would want to make in advance, because the vegetables will only be at their freshest if eaten at once. You can do all the preparation for the dish in advance if you like; then all you will have to do is put it together and bake it. Only about 310 calories per serving; a nice low-calorie treat.

CHICKEN FLORENTINE

4 large whole chicken
  breasts, deboned and
  skinned
1½ tsp. of Chicken
  Seasoning Mix (see index
  for recipe)
¼ cup of flour
2 large eggs, beaten
3 tbsp. of peanut oil
1 pound of fresh spinach
water to cover spinach
1 tsp. of salt
¼ tsp. of Tabasco sauce
1 medium onion, julienned

1 clove of garlic, minced
2 tbsp. of unsalted butter
¼ cup of freshly grated
  Parmesan cheese
4 slices of well-aged Swiss
  cheese
1 tbsp. of flour
½ cup of dry white wine
½ cup of Chicken Stock
  (see index for recipe) or
  chicken broth
juice of half a lemon
¼ tsp. of Tabasco sauce

Wash the chicken breasts and pat them dry with paper towels. Season each chicken breast equally with 1 teaspoon of the Chicken Seasoning Mix and set aside. Mix the ¼ cup of flour and the ½ teaspoon of Chicken Seasoning Mix. Coat each piece of chicken with the seasoned flour and shake off the excess. Dip the coated chicken into the beaten egg and recoat each piece with the flour.

In a heavy skillet that will hold all 4 breasts, heat the peanut oil to hot over medium heat. Fry each breast for about 10 minutes on each side, taking care not to let the chicken stick to the bottom. Once you have started to fry the chicken, place the spinach in a large pot and cover it with water. Add the salt and ¼ teaspoon of Tabasco sauce to the water and bring to a boil over high heat. Boil for 7 minutes, then drain and let the spinach cool. Chop the spinach.

In another heavy skillet, melt the butter over medium heat and sauté the onions and garlic for 5 minutes. Add the chopped spinach and sauté for 4 minutes. Remove from the heat and set aside for later use. When the chicken is fried, place it in a shallow baking dish large enough to hold all 4 breasts. Cover the breasts with the spinach-onion mixture. Sprinkle with the Parmesan cheese and cover each breast with a slice of Swiss cheese. Bake for 12 to 15 minutes at 350 degrees.

While the chicken is baking, add the flour to the skillet in which you fried the chicken and mix it with the pan drippings. Place it over medium heat and cook the flour, stirring constantly, for 3 minutes; this will make a light roux. Add the wine, Chicken Stock, lemon juice, and remaining ¼ teaspoon of Tabasco sauce and blend well. Cook until the sauce thickens. When the chicken is baked, place it on a warm plate and cover generously with the sauce. Serve hot. Serves 4 to 8.

Lagniappe: This dish is best just after it is cooked, but it does lend itself nicely to freezing. I would suggest freezing it in 1-breast portions covered with sauce; this makes it easier to handle and to serve. Thaw in the refrigerator and bake at 300 degrees for 15 minutes.

You can also refrigerate the dish after it is made, keeping the sauce and the chicken separate. Heat the sauce up and cover the chicken with it after you have reheated the chicken in the oven as directed for the frozen portions. If you serve a whole breast per person (4 servings), there are about 770 calories per serving. To serve ½ breast per person (8 servings), each serving will have about 385 calories.

CHICKEN SAUCE LA PRÉE

2 young fryers (2 to 2½ pounds each)
1½ tsp. of Chicken Seasoning Mix (see index for recipe)
3 tbsp. of unsalted butter
2 medium onions, chopped
1 cup of chopped celery
2 cloves of garlic, minced
2 tbsp. of flour
4 large tomatoes, skinned and chopped
1 large bell pepper, chopped
¼ cup of chopped pimento
2 bay leaves
½ tsp. of sweet basil
¼ tsp. of thyme
½ tsp. of salt
½ tsp. of Tabasco sauce
1 tbsp. of Worcestershire sauce
¼ cup of dry red wine
2 cups of Chicken Stock (see index for recipe) or chicken broth
cooked white rice

Wash the fryers well and pat them dry with paper towels. Cut the fryers into serving pieces and season the pieces equally with the Chicken Seasoning Mix. In a large skillet, melt the butter over medium heat and fry the pieces of chicken until each is golden brown on all sides. Place the chicken on a platter for later use.

Add the onions, celery, and garlic to the skillet and sauté over medium heat until the vegetables are lightly browned, about 5 minutes. Add the flour and cook, stirring constantly, until the roux is medium brown. Add the tomatoes, bell pepper, pimento, bay leaves, sweet basil, thyme, and salt. Blend well, then put the chicken back into the skillet. Reduce the heat to low and simmer the chicken in the skillet for about 15 minutes, turning the chicken often to prevent sticking.

Add the Tabasco sauce, Worcestershire sauce, wine, and Chicken Stock and stir until the sauce is smooth. Continue to simmer for 45 minutes to 1 hour longer or until the chicken is tender. Serve hot over cooked white rice with plenty of Sauce la Prée. Serves 8.

Lagniappe: This is a make-ahead dish. You can cook this dish completely and refrigerate or freeze it for later use. To reheat, just thaw in the refrigerator if frozen and heat in a heavy skillet over low heat until the chicken is hot, about 15 to 20 minutes. Making this dish in advance and placing it in the refrigerator seems to improve the flavor, not harm it. Without rice there are only about 295 calories per serving; with ½ cup of cooked white rice, only about 407 calories per serving.

CHICKEN JAMBALAYA

2 medium fryers (2 pounds each)
¼ cup of peanut oil
2 tsp. of Chicken Seasoning Mix (see index for recipe)
1 cup of baked ham, cut into cubes
1 pound of pure pork sausage, sliced into ½-inch-thick circles
2 large onions, chopped
2 medium bell peppers, chopped
1½ cups of chopped celery
3 cloves of garlic, minced

1 14½-ounce can of stewed tomatoes
½ tsp. of Tabasco sauce
1 tsp. of salt
½ tsp. of black pepper
½ tsp. of white pepper
½ tsp. of garlic powder
½ tsp. of onion powder
5 cups of cooked white rice
½ cup of Chicken Stock (see index for recipe) or chicken broth
½ cup of minced fresh parsley
¾ cup of chopped green onion tops

Cut the fryers into 5 equal serving pieces each. In a large, heavy skillet that has a cover, heat the oil over medium heat. Wash each piece of chicken and pat dry with a paper towel. Season with the Chicken Seasoning Mix. Fry each piece in the hot oil until the chicken is well browned. Remove from the skillet and set aside.

Fry the ham in the skillet until it is lightly browned. Remove and place with the chicken. Fry the sausage until it has given up most of its fat and is nicely browned. Remove and place with the chicken and ham. Remove about 2 tablespoons of grease from the skillet. Add the onions, bell peppers, celery, and garlic. Sauté for 5 to 7 minutes or until lightly browned. This will make the onions somewhat sweet.

Now add the tomatoes (without the juice—set this aside) to the skillet and sauté them for 3 minutes. Put the chicken, ham, and sausage back into the skillet. Cover and cook over low heat for 25 minutes, stirring every once and a while to prevent sticking. Add the Tabasco sauce, salt, black pepper, white pepper, garlic powder, onion powder, and the juice from the tomato can. Blend well. Add the rice and Chicken Stock; blend very well.

Cover and simmer over very low heat for 25 more minutes, stirring often. Add the parsley and green onion tops and mix well. Cook, uncovered, for 3 more minutes. Serve hot. Serves 10.

Lagniappe: This dish can be completely cooked in advance and refrigerated or frozen. To reheat, thaw in the refrigerator if frozen, place in a covered baking dish, and bake at 300 degrees for 12 to 15 minutes. Or you can put it frozen into the microwave and heat at 100 percent power for 5 minutes, then at 80 percent for 5 to 7 minutes or until heated through. This is an excellent one-dish meal. About 480 calories per serving.

CHICKEN CREPES TERRIAU

1½ pounds of chicken breast meat
1 tsp. of Chicken Seasoning Mix (see index for recipe)
1 stick of unsalted butter
1 cup of chopped onion
½ cup of chopped bell pepper
2 cloves of garlic, minced
½ cup of finely chopped celery
½ cup of chopped green onion bottoms
½ cup of flour
1½ cups of Chicken Stock (see index for recipe) or chicken broth
1 cup of dry white wine
1½ cups of milk
½ cup of evaporated milk
10 large mushrooms, sliced
¼ cup of minced fresh parsley
¼ cup of chopped green onion tops
1 tsp. of salt
½ tsp. of Tabasco sauce
¼ tsp. of black pepper
¼ tsp. of white pepper
1 tbsp. of fresh lemon juice
2 large eggs, well beaten
1 recipe Crepes (see index for recipe)
butter to grease baking pan
½ cup of light cream
Hollandaise Sauce (see index for recipe)
paprika

Wash the chicken meat and pat it dry. Season equally with the Chicken Seasoning Mix. Place in a broiling pan and broil in the broiler about 4 inches from the heat for 7 minutes on each side. Remove and let cool. Chop half of the meat very fine and the other half coarse. Set aside.

Melt the butter in a large heavy skillet. Sauté the onion, bell pepper, garlic, celery, and green onion bottoms in the skillet until limp and lightly browned, about 5 minutes. Add the flour and blend it in well. Cook, stirring constantly, for 4 minutes over medium-low heat. Add the Chicken Stock and wine and blend in well. Whip in the milk and evaporated milk with a wire whisk. Add the chicken, mushrooms, parsley, green onion tops, salt, Tabasco sauce, black pepper, white pepper, and lemon juice and cook over medium-low heat, stirring constantly, until the sauce thickens and is smooth.

Place the eggs in a mixing bowl and add a large spoonful of the thickened sauce to the egg mixture. Stir well. Add one more large spoonful of sauce and stir well, then pour the egg mixture into the skillet and blend it in well. Spoon about ¼ cup of the sauce down the middle of each crepe and roll each crepe. (There will be sauce left in the pot.)

Place filled crepes in a lightly greased baking pan. Add the light cream to the remaining sauce and blend well. Keep this sauce warm over very low heat. Bake the crepes for 10 minutes at 350 degrees. Remove the pan from the oven and set 2 crepes on each plate. Top crepes with chicken cream sauce, 1 tablespoon of Hollandaise Sauce, and a light dusting of paprika. Serve at once. Serves 6.

Lagniappe: This is a real company dish, yet it is very economical. You can make the crepes all the way to the baking stage and refrigerate or freeze them for later use; just cover them tightly. To reheat, thaw them in the refrigerator if frozen and bake for 15 minutes at 350 degrees. You can also freeze the chicken sauce that is left to top the dish; freeze it before you add the light cream, then thaw in the refrigerator when ready to serve and proceed as above. Do not put the dish together completely, including the Hollandaise Sauce, and try to refrigerate or freeze. It won't work!

You can substitute leftover baked turkey and make **Turkey Crepes Terriau;** just follow the directions as above. Six servings of 2 crepes each have about 795 calories per serving without the Hollandaise Sauce; with the sauce, about 915 calories per serving. To reduce the calories and still have a nice serving, just serve 1 crepe for a calorie count of about 398 without the Hollandaise or 458 calories with the Hollandaise.

FRIED CHICKEN

1 large fryer (3½ to 4
pounds), cut into serving
pieces
2 tsp. of Chicken Seasoning
Mix (see index for recipe)
1 cup of mustard
2 eggs, beaten
½ cup of light cream

½ tsp. of Tabasco sauce
½ tsp. of salt
1 tsp. of finely minced fresh
parsley
½ cup of flour
1 tsp. of cornstarch
2 cups of peanut oil

Wash the fryer parts well and pat them dry with a paper towel.
Season all pieces equally with 1 teaspoon of the Chicken Seasoning
Mix. Place the chicken in a large glass bowl and add the mustard,
mixing so that all the pieces are coated. Cover the bowl with plastic
wrap and refrigerate for at least 2 hours (or up to 24). Remove the
chicken and shake off any excess mustard.

Combine in a large mixing bowl the eggs, cream, Tabasco sauce,
salt, and parsley; beat until well blended. Combine in another bowl
the flour, cornstarch, and the other teaspoon of Chicken Seasoning
Mix until well blended. Dip each piece of chicken into the egg
mixture, then coat it with the flour mixture and place it on a platter.
Repeat until all pieces of chicken are coated.

Heat the peanut oil in a heavy skillet to about 350 degrees. Add
the pieces of chicken one at a time (largest pieces of dark meat first)
until all are in the skillet. Cook until both sides of each piece are a
crisp golden brown, about 12 minutes after the last piece has been
added. Serve hot. Serves 6.

Lagniappe: Do not freeze or refrigerate the chicken after cooking if
you want a crispy product. You can proceed with the recipe all
the way to dipping it into the flour, then cover it all and set it in
the refrigerator until you are ready to fry it. About 400 calories
per serving.

EASY OVEN-FRIED CHICKEN

1 large fryer (about 3½
  pounds), cut into serving
  pieces
1 cup of buttermilk
½ tsp. of Tabasco sauce
1 cup of dried French bread
  crumbs

2 tsp. of Chicken
  Seasoning Mix (see
  index for recipe)
1 tbsp. of flour
butter to grease baking dish

Wash chicken pieces and pat dry with paper towels. Place chicken in a glass dish. Mix the buttermilk and Tabasco sauce and pour it over the chicken. Let it sit, covered, in the refrigerator overnight.

Mix the bread crumbs, Chicken Seasoning Mix, and flour in a large glass bowl. Roll each piece of chicken in the crumb mixture, pressing the chicken into the mixture firmly to get as much coating on the chicken as possible. Place the chicken parts in a lightly greased baking dish and bake, uncovered, for 1 hour at 350 degrees. Turn the chicken carefully twice during the baking process. The chicken should be crisp on the outside and juicy on the inside. Serve at once. Serves 8.

Lagniappe: Do not freeze or refrigerate after baking. You can get the chicken ready to bake and place it in the refrigerator for up to 10 hours before you bake it, but do not attempt to reheat it after baking. It will be soggy and will have lost much of the juiciness it had coming from the oven. About 291 calories per serving. Not much you can do to reduce the calories, but this count is not really too bad for your main-dish meat.

POULET GERMAIN

2 whole chicken breasts, skinned, deboned, and diced (1¼ pounds of meat)
¼ cup of peanut oil
¾ stick of butter, cut into pats
¼ cup of finely chopped onion
1 bunch of green onions, chopped
¼ cup of chopped celery
1 large bell pepper, cut into thin strips
2 large tomatoes, cut into thin wedges, skin on
8 large fresh mushrooms, sliced
2½ cups of cooked white rice
¼ cup of broken toasted pecans
¼ cup of minced fresh parsley
1 tsp. of salt
½ tsp. of Tabasco sauce
¼ tsp. of black pepper
½ tsp. of fresh lemon juice

Wash the chicken and pat dry with paper towels. Arrange all ingredients in the order listed; you will need to have them handy. In a very large, heavy skillet over medium-high heat, heat the oil until it is very hot. Add the butter pats and stir through until they melt. Add the chicken and onion and sauté for 3 minutes. The chicken pieces should be white in the centers and beginning to brown around the edges.

Add the green onions and coat them well with the pan liquid. Add the celery and bell pepper and sauté for 1 minute. Add the tomatoes and stir them through, making sure they are well coated. Add the mushrooms and stir them through; the slices should darken some- what as the liquid coats them. Add the rice and blend it in well. Add the pecans and parsley and blend well. Add the salt, Tabasco sauce, black pepper, and lemon juice and blend well. Serve hot. Serves 6 to 8.

Lagniappe: This is such an easy and quick dish that you don't have to worry about freezing or refrigerating. Do not make this in advance. All you can do is get all of the ingredients ready in separate bowls, then just line them up and go right before you are ready to serve. This wonderful one-dish meal only takes about 10 minutes to cook (not counting preparing the chicken and cooking the rice), so you can serve it without much worry and planning.

A nice fruit salad with poppy seed dressing complements this dish well. Six servings only have about 400 calories each, and 8 servings have only about 300 calories each. Not only delicious, but low-calorie as well!

POULET NICHOLLI

2 tbsp. of flour
1½ tsp. of Chicken
  Seasoning Mix (see index
  for recipe)
1 large fryer (3 to 4 pounds),
  cut into 6 serving pieces
½ stick of unsalted butter

½ cup of cream sherry
1¼ cup of half-and-half
¼ tsp. of Tabasco sauce
¼ tsp. of lemon juice
1 tsp. of Worcestershire
  sauce

Mix the flour with the Chicken Seasoning Mix. Coat the chicken pieces thoroughly and equally with the seasoned flour. Melt the butter in a skillet over medium heat. Add the coated pieces of chicken and fry until the chicken is well browned on all sides. Reduce the heat to low and cook the chicken until it is tender and cooked, about 25 minutes. (Be sure to turn the chicken three or four times during cooking to cook it on both sides.)

Place the chicken on a heated platter and place the platter in a 200-degree oven to await the sauce. Turn the heat under the skillet to medium again. As the skillet gets hot, add the sherry; it should sizzle. When the temperature drops (you will note the bubbles subsiding), add the half-and-half, Tabasco sauce, lemon juice, and Worcestershire sauce. Stir until the sauce is well blended and smooth; it should also thicken. Remove the chicken from the oven and cover liberally with the sauce. Serve hot. Serves 6.

Lagniappe: Do not freeze this dish. For best results, make it just before you are ready to serve it. It does not refrigerate well, either. About the only thing you can do in advance is season the chicken and place it in the refrigerator until you are ready to begin, although this does not save that much time in preparation. Under 400 calories per serving.

CHICKEN AND BROCCOLI QUICHE

1 unbaked 9-inch deep-dish pie shell
1½ cups of chopped cooked chicken
1 cup of cooked fresh broccoli flowerets
2 tbsp. of toasted slivered almonds
1 cup of grated mild Cheddar cheese
1 cup of grated Swiss cheese

1 cup of milk (substitute half-and-half for a richer quiche)
3 large eggs, well beaten
½ tsp. of Tabasco sauce
1 tsp. of Worcestershire sauce
½ tsp. of salt
¼ tsp. of black pepper
1 tbsp. of finely minced fresh parsley

Allow the pie shell to stand at room temperature. Mix the chicken, broccoli, and almonds and pour the mixture into the unbaked shell. Mix the two cheeses well, then sprinkle them over the chicken and broccoli. Beat the remaining ingredients together for 1 minute with a wire whisk and pour into the pie shell.

Bake for 30 minutes at 375 degrees or until a knife inserted into the center comes out clean. Let the quiche stand and cool for about 5 minutes. Serve hot. Serves 6.

Lagniappe: You'll like what you can do with quiche. It can be completely baked, then frozen or refrigerated. You can slice a few pieces from the quiche, then put it into the refrigerator for later use. It reheats beautifully in the microwave, or you can reheat it in the oven at 350 degrees for about 7 minutes.

Fruit salad is a nice accompaniment. You can also do many different things with this one simple recipe. Here are a few. Change the chicken to 1 cup of diced ham, change the broccoli to 1 cup of diced fresh tomatoes, and add ½ cup of chopped onion, and you have **Quiche Lorraine.** To make **Quiche Dupris,** leave the chicken in but substitute 1 cup of fresh asparagus spears for the broccoli and add 2 tablespoons of chopped onion. Change the chicken, broccoli, and almonds while leaving the rest of the recipe intact and create your own quiche!

About 467 calories per serving for the chicken and broccoli, about 750 per serving for Quiche Lorraine, and about 462 per serving for Quiche Dupris.

CHICKEN CORDON BLEU

6 chicken breast halves, deboned
2 tsp. of Chicken Seasoning Mix (see index for recipe)
2 large (1-ounce) slices of aged cheddar cheese
2 large (1-ounce) slices of aged Swiss cheese
2 large (1-ounce) slices of baked ham

1 cup of dried bread crumbs
2 tbsp. of flour
1 large egg, well beaten
1 tsp. of Worcestershire sauce
¼ tsp. of Tabasco sauce
3 tbsp. of half-and-half
¼ cup of peanut oil
2 tbsp. of butter

Butterfly the chicken by cutting into the center of the breast about half way through. Spread the meat apart with your fingers as much as possible. Season the chicken breasts equally with 1 teaspoon of Chicken Seasoning Mix. Using a kitchen mallet, pound the chicken breasts until they are about ⅜ of an inch thick.

Cut the cheese slices and ham slices into thirds. Place a piece of cheddar cheese in the center of a flattened chicken breast. Top the cheddar with a piece of ham and a piece of Swiss cheese. Fold the chicken around the ham and cheeses and seal the edges. Mold it tightly with your hands to seal the edges together. Repeat the process for the other chicken breasts.

Mix the bread crumbs, the other teaspoon of Chicken Seasoning Mix, and the flour in a large mixing bowl. Mix the egg, Worcestershire sauce, Tabasco sauce, and half-and-half in another bowl. Dip the filled chicken breasts into the egg mixture, then roll them in the bread crumbs. Repeat for the remaining chicken breasts.

Heat the oil in a heavy skillet over medium-low heat until it is hot. Add the butter and allow it to melt, then add the chicken breasts. Sauté until they are browned on all sides. Remove from the skillet and drain on paper towels. Serve at once. Serves 6.

Lagniappe: After you sauté the breasts, do not reheat to serve again. You'll lose too much of the quality and texture. You can, however, do everything up to frying the chicken and place it in the refrigerator for up to 10 hours before you are ready to sauté. This will save you a lot of preparation time.

This is an excellent company dish and can be used with many variations. To make **Chicken Kiev,** just substitute the following mixture for the cheese and ham inside the chicken breasts:

> 1 cup of softened unsalted butter
> 1 tbsp. of minced green onion tops
> 2 tbsp. of minced fresh parsley
> ½ tsp. of Chicken Seasoning Mix (see index for recipe)
> 1 tsp. of white wine
> ¼ tsp. of Tabasco Sauce

Mix ingredients well, then refrigerate until the butter has hardened somewhat, about 1 hour. Mold the mixture into 6 equal flat parts that are in the same shape as one side of a flattened chicken breast. Wrap individually in plastic wrap and freeze for 1 hour. Place as you would the ham and cheeses in the original recipe and proceed as directed. This is an excellent variation. About 480 calories per serving of the Cordon Bleu and about 646 calories per serving of the Kiev.

CHICKEN EUPHROSINE

4 cups of cooked chicken,
cut into bite-size pieces
2 cups of diced, lightly
toasted French bread
1 cup of chopped onion
1 cup of chopped celery
¼ cup of diced bell pepper
3 tbsp. of diced pimento
2 cloves of garlic, minced
½ cup of Chicken Stock
(see index for recipe) or
chicken broth
½ cup of milk
½ cup of mayonnaise
½ pound of Gruyère cheese,
grated

¼ pound of Swiss cheese,
grated
1 10¾-ounce can of cream
of mushroom soup
½ tsp. of Tabasco sauce
½ tsp. of salt
1 tsp. of Worcestershire
sauce
1 cup of cooked white rice
¼ cup of chopped green
onion tops
paprika
¼ cup of minced fresh
parsley

Preheat the oven to 350 degrees. Combine all ingredients except the paprika and parsley. Pour the mixture into a 2½-quart baking dish and sprinkle the top with the paprika. Bake at 350 degrees for 1 hour. Sprinkle the top with the fresh parsley and serve hot. Serves 8.

Lagniappe: This is a great dish for leftovers. You can serve it at once, refrigerate it uncooked to cook later, or completely bake it and refrigerate or freeze. To reheat, just thaw in the refrigerator if frozen and bake at 350 degrees until hot, about 12 to 15 minutes. Then top with parsley.

You can make the same dish with other leftover meats. Use your leftover turkey and make **Turkey Euphrosine.** Use your leftover pork chops and make **Pork Euphrosine.** Ham also makes a nice dish called **Ham Euphrosine.** The calories per serving of each version are as follows: chicken—about 380; turkey—about 397; ham—about 517; and pork—about 425.

CHICKEN ROSEMARY

1 large fryer or roasting
chicken (3½ to 4 pounds)
½ tsp. of Chicken
Seasoning Mix (see index
for recipe)
1 small onion, sliced
1 red apple, cored but
unpeeled, cut into thin
slices

½ stalk of celery, chopped
into large pieces
½ strip of bacon
1 tbsp. of butter, softened
1½ tsp. of Chicken
Seasoning Mix (see index)
1 tsp. of rosemary
½ cup of water
½ cup of red wine vinegar

Wash the chicken and pat it dry with paper towels. Preheat the oven to 425 degrees. Season the inside of the chicken cavity with the ½ teaspoon of Chicken Seasoning Mix. Place the onion, apple, celery, and bacon inside the cavity. Truss the chicken legs by pulling them through pieces of the skin at the cavity opening so that both legs are secure; simply cut a small slit through the skin on each side of the chicken and tuck the crossed legs through the slits. Rub the softened butter into the chicken with your hands, then season with the 1½ teaspoons of Chicken Seasoning Mix and the rosemary.

Place the chicken in a baking dish and bake for 20 minutes at 425 degrees, then reduce the heat to 350 degrees and bake for 1 hour and 15 minutes. When the chicken is done, remove it from the oven and place it on a warm platter. Pour off any excess fat from the pan and deglaze the pan with the water and wine vinegar, making sure to dissolve all the pan drippings. Slice the warm chicken and spoon the sauce over it. Serve warm. Serves 8.

Lagniappe: This dish is best served right after it is cooked. You can refrigerate or freeze leftovers for later use, but don't miss out on the excellent flavors and textures of the chicken and sauce right after they are prepared. To reheat the leftovers, thaw in the refrigerator if frozen and bake at 350 degrees, covered, until the chicken is heated, about 12 minutes. About 235 calories per serving if you use a fryer and about 483 calories per serving with a roasting chicken.

CHICKEN AND RICE CASSEROLE

2 whole large chicken breasts, skinned and deboned
1 tsp. of Chicken Seasoning Mix (see index for recipe)
¼ cup of peanut oil
3½ tbsp. of flour
1 8-ounce can of tomato sauce
1 large onion, chopped
1 medium bell pepper, chopped
2 cloves of garlic, minced
1 stalk of celery, chopped
2 cups of Chicken Stock (see index for recipe) or chicken broth

1½ cups of cooked white rice
½ cup of chopped green onion tops
¼ cup of minced fresh parsley
1 tsp. of salt
¼ tsp. of Tabasco sauce
¼ tsp. of black pepper
¼ tsp. of white pepper
butter to grease baking dish
¼ cup of dry bread crumbs
2 pats of butter, cut into pieces

Wash the chicken breasts and pat them dry with a paper towel. Using a sharp, heavy knife, cut the breasts into bite-size pieces (strips are nice). Place them in a bowl and season them with the Chicken Seasoning Mix. In a large, heavy pot, heat the oil over medium heat. Sauté the chicken pieces for 5 to 7 minutes until they are lightly browned. Remove the chicken from the oil and set aside.

Add the flour to the oil and make a medium-dark roux by heating the flour, stirring constantly, over medium-low heat until it is reddish-brown. Add the tomato sauce, onion, bell pepper, garlic, celery, and Chicken Stock and bring to a hard boil. Reduce the heat and simmer for 10 minutes, then add the chicken and simmer for 10 minutes. Add the rice, stir well, and simmer for 5 minutes. Add the green onion tops, parsley, salt, Tabasco sauce, black pepper, and white pepper. Mix well and pour into a lightly greased baking dish.

Sprinkle with the bread crumbs and dot with butter. Bake at 350 degrees for 20 minutes. Serve hot. Serves 6.

Lagniappe: This is a wonderful make-ahead dish. You can refrigerate it or freeze it, either before or after baking. To reheat, just thaw in the refrigerator if frozen and bake at 350 degrees for 20 minutes or until hot. If the dish is merely refrigerated, bake it for 15 minutes instead of 20.

I find that freezing it after baking seems to do better than freezing it before baking. Baking tends to drive off some of the water that is retained in the dish during the freezing process. About 315 calories per serving.

SAUTÉED CHICKEN LIVERS PERRON

1 pound of fresh chicken livers
1½ tsp. of Chicken Seasoning Mix (see index for recipe)
2 strips of bacon, chopped
2 tbsp. of unsalted butter
1 small onion, sliced in wedges
1 small bell pepper, cut into thin slices
1 clove of garlic, minced
½ cup of dry red wine
2 tbsp. of fresh lemon juice
¼ cup of heavy cream
¼ tsp. of Tabasco sauce

Season the chicken livers with the Chicken Seasoning Mix and set them aside. Fry the bacon in a skillet over medium heat until it is crisp and brown. Add the butter and melt, then add the chicken livers and sauté them for 3 minutes, being careful not to tear the livers. Remove the livers from the skillet. Add the onion, bell pepper, and garlic and sauté for 5 minutes.

Return the livers to the skillet, reduce the heat, and simmer for 15 minutes. Remove the livers from the skillet and add the wine and lemon juice to deglaze the pan drippings. Raise the heat to high and reduce the liquid by about one-third, then remove from the heat. Add the cream and Tabasco sauce and blend through. Serve the livers hot with plenty of cream sauce. Serves 4.

Lagniappe: Do not freeze or refrigerate this dish. The liver will break apart if you try any more handling of it. The sauce is also excellent over a fresh baked potato or over stiff mashed potatoes. Another serving suggestion is to serve this over toast points or a lightly toasted piece of French bread.

Only about 383 calories per serving. Over half of a medium baked potato, there are about 456 calories per serving; over ½ cup of mashed potatoes, about 452 calories; and over 1 slice of bread cut into toast points, about 437 calories.

ROASTED CORNISH HEN THEOGENE

For roasting the hens before stuffing:

4 small Rock Cornish hens
(1 pound each)

2 tsp. of Chicken Seasoning
Mix (see index for recipe)
melted butter

For the stuffing:

2 tbsp. of butter
1 tbsp. of olive oil
½ pound of fresh chicken
livers
½ pound of ham, diced
1 clove of garlic, minced
1 stalk of celery, minced
¼ cup of chopped bell
pepper
½ cup of chopped green
onions

1½ cups of diced French
bread
milk
½ tsp. of salt
½ tsp. of Tabasco sauce
¼ tsp. of black pepper
¼ tsp. of white pepper
½ tsp. of sweet basil
3 tbsp. of minced fresh
parsley
melted butter

For the sauce:

1 tbsp. of flour
½ cup of chopped onion
½ cup of Chicken Stock
(see index for recipe)
½ cup of heavy cream
¼ cup of brandy

¼ tsp. of Tabasco sauce
½ tsp. of salt
¼ tsp. of white pepper
1 tbsp. of finely minced
fresh parsley
⅛ tsp. of ground bay leaves

To roast the hens:

Preheat the oven to 475 degrees. Wash the hens and pat them dry with a paper towel. Season them well with the Chicken Seasoning Mix and arrange them in a heavy baking dish. Brush them with melted butter and roast at 475 degrees for 10 minutes, then remove them from the oven and allow them to cool. Reduce the oven temperature to 425 degrees.

To prepare the stuffing:

In a large, heavy skillet, melt the butter over medium heat and add the olive oil. Add the chicken livers and ham and sauté over medium heat for 5 minutes, then lower the heat to low and add the garlic, celery, bell pepper, and green onion. Sauté for 15 minutes, stirring often.

Meanwhile, place the French bread in a large bowl and add enough milk to cover it; let the bread soak. When it is soaked, squeeze the excess milk from the bread with your hands and set the bread aside. When the liver-ham mixture is through sautéing, add the soaked bread, salt, Tabasco sauce, black pepper, white pepper, sweet basil, and parsley. Blend well and break up the liver as much as possible. Spoon equal amounts of the stuffing mix into each hen and truss the legs together. Brush the hens with more melted butter and bake at 425 degrees for 30 minutes. Remove the baking dish from the oven. Take the hens out of the baking dish and keep them warm in the oven.

To make the sauce:

Remove any excess fat from the baking dish. Add the flour and blend well. Cook over low heat for 3 minutes, then add the onion and sauté for 3 minutes. Add the Chicken Stock and blend well. Remove from the heat and add the heavy cream, brandy, Tabasco sauce, salt, white pepper, parsley, and bay leaves. Blend well, then return to the heat and cook, stirring constantly, until the sauce begins to bubble and thicken. Remove the hens from the oven and place a hen on each of 4 plates. Spoon the cream sauce generously over each hen and serve at once. Serves 4 or 8.

Lagniappe: Sorry, but there is no way to freeze or refrigerate this dish. The only think you can do in advance is roast the hens the first time, make the stuffing, and stuff the birds. At this point you can refrigerate to cook later. This will save you a lot of preparation time when you are ready to serve. In order for your sauce to have the effect you need, don't attempt to make it in advance!

If you serve 1 whole hen per person, the calorie count is about 1,004 per serving. If you split each hen right down the center and give each person half of the stuffing to go with half of a hen, you can serve 8 people for about 502 calories per person.

ROAST TURKEY WITH OYSTER DRESSING

1 12- to 15-pound turkey, thawed and left at room temperature for 2 hours
1½ tsp. of Chicken Seasoning Mix (see index for recipe)
1 recipe of Oyster Dressing (see index for recipe)
2½ tsp. of Chicken Seasoning Mix (see index)
2 tbsp. of softened butter
½ cup of cognac
½ stick of butter, melted
¼ tsp. of Tabasco sauce

Preheat the oven to 425 degrees. Rinse the turkey well inside and out with water and pat dry with paper towels. Season the cavity well with 1½ teaspoons of the Chicken Seasoning Mix, then stuff the cavity with the Oyster Dressing. Truss the turkey legs tightly and fold the wings under. Season the outside of the turkey well with the other 2½ teaspoons of the Chicken Seasoning Mix. Rub the outside of the turkey with the softened 2 tablespoons of butter (you'll have to use your hands to get the job done right).

Place the turkey in a roasting pan, breast side up, and bake at 425 degrees for 30 minutes, then reduce the heat to 350 degrees and cook for about 2½ hours. Baste the turkey often with pan drippings during the first hour. Mix the cognac, melted butter, and Tabasco sauce and baste with this mixture for the rest of the cooking time.

When you run out of this basting liquid, use the pan drippings again.

Check for doneness by piercing the turkey with a fork; if the juices run clear, the turkey is done. Allow the turkey to cool for about 15 minutes before you begin to carve it. Serve warm. Serves 15 to 20.

Lagniappe: Turkey should be eaten soon after it is baked for the best flavor and texture. However, many people can't take all the time needed to prepare a turkey before serving. You can bake the turkey completely, slice it, cover it tightly, and either refrigerate it or freeze it. To reheat, just completely thaw in the refrigerator if frozen and bake, covered, for 10 minutes at 350 degrees, then uncover and bake for 5 more minutes.

Remember to remove the stuffing soon after the turkey is taken out of the oven so it will not have time to be exposed to bacteria. You can also remove most of the excess fat from the roasting pan and deglaze the pan drippings with water, wine, or light cream (or any combination of these) to make an excellent gravy.

Fifteen servings have about 624 calories each without dressing and 790 calories with dressing. Twenty servings have about 470 calories each without dressing or 592 calories each with dressing.

QUICK TURKEY JAMBALAYA

1 strip of bacon, chopped
2 tbsp. of butter
2 cups of baked ham, chopped into cubes
2 cups of turkey, chopped into cubes
1 cup of chopped onion
½ cup of chopped bell pepper
½ cup of chopped celery
2 cloves of garlic, minced
1½ cups of raw long-grain rice

6 fresh mushrooms, sliced
3 cups of Chicken Stock (see index for recipe) or chicken broth
1½ tsp. of Chicken Seasoning Mix (see index for recipe)
¼ tsp. of Tabasco sauce
½ cup of finely chopped green onion
¼ cup of minced fresh parsley

In a heavy skillet that has a cover, fry the bacon until it is crisp. Add the butter and melt over medium heat. Sauté the ham and turkey for 4 minutes, then remove the meat from the skillet. Add the onion, bell pepper, celery, and garlic and sauté until the onion is lightly browned, about 5 to 7 minutes. Add the rice and mushrooms and sauté for 3 minutes. Return the meat to the skillet and sauté for 1 minute. Add the Chicken Stock, Chicken Seasoning Mix, and Tabasco sauce.

Cook, uncovered, for 25 to 30 minutes or until the rice is tender. Add the parsley and green onion and mix well. Cover and cook over very low heat for 5 minutes. Serve hot. Serves 6 to 8.

Lagniappe: This dish can be completely made in advance and either refrigerated or frozen for later use. To reheat, just thaw in the refrigerator if frozen and heat, tightly covered, in a heavy skillet over medium-low heat for 5 to 7 minutes until the dish is hot.

This is an excellent way to use leftover ham and turkey after the holidays. I usually freeze my ham and turkey leftovers in a 2-cup container for later use. It also makes a nice dish when the holidays are *not* near! About 530 calories in each of 6 servings and about 397 calories in each of 8 servings.

BAKED DUCK

1 duck (1½ pounds)
1½ tsp. of salt
¼ tsp. of black pepper
¼ tsp. of white pepper
⅛ tsp. of red pepper
¼ tsp. of thyme
¼ tsp. of filé powder
½ cup of flour

¼ cup of peanut oil
1 small onion, cut into
   fourths
1 stalk of celery, chopped
2 cloves of garlic, minced
1 cup of light cream
1 tbsp. of dry white wine

Cut the duck into fourths. Mix the salt, black pepper, white pepper, red pepper, thyme, filé powder, and flour well. Dredge the duck pieces well in this mixture.

In a large, heavy metal pot that has a cover, heat the peanut oil over medium heat. Fry the duck pieces in the oil until they are brown on both sides; this will take about 20 to 25 minutes. Remove from the heat and add the onion, celery, and garlic. Stir through, then pour the cream and wine over the duck. Cover and bake at 350 degrees until the duck is tender, about 45 minutes. Serve hot. Serves 2 to 4.

Lagniappe: You may begin this dish early and stop the process after the duck has been fried. You can then refrigerate it until you are ready to bake. Add about 5 more minutes to the baking time if you do it this way.

About 1,228 calories per serving for 2 servings and about 614 calories per serving for 4 servings.

PAN-ROASTED WILD DUCK

3 wild ducks (1½ to 2 pounds each)
1 large onion, cut into thirds
1 ripe green apple, cut into thirds, seeds removed
1 large tender turnip, cut into thirds
1 carrot, cut into thirds
1 strip of bacon, cut into thirds
1 stalk of celery, cut into thirds

1½ tsp. of Chicken Seasoning Mix (see index for recipe)
3 tbsp. of peanut oil
1 tsp. of Chicken Seasoning Mix (see index)
1 cup of Chicken Stock (see index for recipe) or chicken broth
½ cup of dry white wine
1 cup of water
cooked white rice

Wash the ducks well and pat dry with paper towels. Arrange the onion, apple, turnip, carrot, bacon, and celery in 3 piles, one third of each item in each pile. Season the inside of each duck equally with 1½ teaspoons of Chicken Seasoning Mix, then place a pile of vegetables into the cavity in each duck. Truss the duck closed on both ends. Heat the peanut oil in a heavy metal pot with a cover over medium heat until hot. Season the outside of the ducks equally with the 1 teaspoon of Chicken Seasoning Mix. Fry the first duck for 2 minutes, turning often. Remove and set aside. Repeat the process for the other 2 ducks.

Return all the ducks to the pan. Add the Chicken Stock and wine. Lower the heat to medium-low, cover tightly, and cook for 1½ hours. Remove the cover, raise the heat to medium, and cook until the ducks turn a rich brown. You may have to turn them a few times to get an even brown. When they are well browned, add the water, cover, and cook for 15 more minutes. Serve hot with the gravy over rice. You can also serve the vegetables from the cavity if you like. Serves 6 to 8.

Lagniappe: This dish is great right from the pan, but you can refrigerate or freeze it for later use after cooking it completely. To reheat, just thaw in the refrigerator if frozen and heat in a covered pan for about 12 to 15 minutes or until the ducks are heated through. You can add a little extra water if the gravy gets too low. When you serve the dish, placing the ducks on a platter surrounded by the vegetables from the cavity makes a nice presentation.

Six servings without rice have about 616 calories each; with ½ cup of cooked rice, about 828 calories each. Eight servings without rice have about 462 calories each; with rice, about 574 calories each.

STUFFED DOVES HYPPOLITE

2 strips of bacon, chopped
1 medium onion, chopped
1 medium bell pepper, chopped
2 cloves of garlic, minced
3 tbsp. of minced celery
3 tbsp. of minced carrots
¼ cup of finely minced fresh apple
¼ cup of finely diced ham
1 cup of finely diced soft French bread
6 doves, cleaned and split down the back

1½ tsp. of Chicken Seasoning Mix (see index for recipe)
¼ cup of Chicken Stock (see index for recipe) or chicken broth
1 large egg, lightly beaten
3 tbsp. of white wine
½ tsp. of Tabasco sauce
½ tsp. of salt
¼ tsp. of garlic powder
¼ tsp. of onion powder
½ tsp. of sweet basil
6 strips of bacon

In a heavy skillet over medium heat, fry the chopped bacon strips until browned. Add the onion, bell pepper, garlic, celery, and carrots and sauté for 5 minutes. Add the apple and ham and sauté for 2 minutes. Add the French bread and mix well, then remove from the heat and set aside to cool.

Season the doves equally with the Chicken Seasoning Mix and set them aside. Add to the French bread mixture the Chicken Stock, egg, wine, Tabasco sauce, salt, garlic powder, onion powder, and sweet basil and mix well. Stuff each dove equally with the stuffing mixture until all of it has been used. Wrap a strip of bacon around each bird to hold the stuffing inside and secure the bacon with a toothpick.

Place in an ungreased shallow baking dish and bake for 1 hour at 325 degrees. Baste the doves 3 times with the pan juices during the cooking process. Serve hot. Serves 6.

Lagniappe: This dish is wonderful right from the oven, but it can be made in advance and stored in the refrigerator for up to 3 days or frozen for later use. To reheat, thaw in the refrigerator if frozen and bake at 325 degrees for 15 minutes, basting the doves twice. You can also use small ducks instead of doves and make **Stuffed Ducks Hyppolite.** About 670 calories per serving. I do not suggest any calorie reduction for this recipe.

QUAIL EULALIE

6 quail, cleaned and split in half
1½ tsp. of Chicken Seasoning Mix (see index for recipe)
1 stick of unsalted butter
1½ tbsp. of flour
½ cup of finely chopped onion
1 stalk of celery, minced

1 tbsp. of minced bell pepper
1 clove of garlic, minced
1 cup of dry white wine
¼ cup of Chicken Stock (see index for recipe) or chicken broth
¼ tsp. of tarragon
3 tbsp. of red wine vinegar

Season the quail halves evenly with the Chicken Seasoning Mix. In a large skillet that has a cover, melt the butter over medium heat and sauté the quail halves until they are lightly browned. Remove the quail to a warm platter. Reduce the heat to low and add the flour. Make a light roux by blending the flour into the butter and pan drippings and cooking for 3 minutes. Be sure to cover all parts of the skillet while stirring or whisking. Add the onion, celery, bell pepper, and garlic and sauté for 5 minutes.

Raise the heat to medium, then add the wine, Chicken Stock, and tarragon. Blend well and bring to a boil. Place the quail back in the skillet, reduce the heat to simmer, cover, and cook for about 20 minutes. Add the wine vinegar and blend well. Continue to cook, uncovered, for 15 minutes or until the quail are tender. Serve hot. Serves 6 or 12.

Lagniappe: This dish can be made completely and frozen for later use. You can also prepare most of it ahead and store it in the refrigerator until your guests arrive or until you are ready for dinner. If you want to use the dish later on the same day, cook it through the blending-in of the vinegar, then remove from the heat and cover. Let it cool for 10 minutes before placing it in the refrigerator. When you are about ready to serve the dish, heat it on high heat until it comes to a boil, then reduce the heat to simmer and cook for 15 minutes.

If you freeze the dish, cook it completely and freeze it with its pan juices. To reheat, thaw it in the refrigerator, then place it in the oven, covered, and bake it for 15 minutes at 350 degrees. If the serving is 1 quail per person (6 servings), there are about 876 calories per serving. For ½ quail per person (12 servings), there are about 438 calories per serving.

Meats

CAJUN PAN-FRIED BEEF RIBEYE STEAK

4 ribeye steaks, about
¾ pound each

6 tsp. of Beef Seasoning Mix
(see index for recipe)
3 tbsp. of peanut oil

Season each of the ribeyes with about 1½ teaspoons of the Beef Seasoning Mix, pushing the seasoning into the meat with the palm of your hand.

In a very heavy old black iron pot, heat the peanut oil over high heat. When the oil begins to smoke, add the first ribeye and cook it 2 minutes on each side for medium rare. Be sure to have your stove hood fan on full, as this will smoke quite a lot. Remove it to a hot plate, cover the plate with aluminum foil, and place it in a warm (175-degree) oven. Repeat the process until you have cooked all 4 steaks. The bottom of the steaks will look black, but the steaks will be quite juicy and will not taste burnt at all. Serve at once. Serves 4.

Lagniappe: Nothing you can do in advance for this dish, but it cooks so quickly that you won't need much preparation time. If you want your steaks rare, cook them about 1½ minutes on each side, and cook them last so you won't have to put them into the oven to keep them warm. If you want them medium, cook them about 3 minutes on each side. If you want them medium well, cook them about 4 minutes on each side. If you want them well done (shame on you), cook them about 5 minutes on each side and cook them first so they will sit longer in the oven while you are cooking the others.

You can use sirloin strips instead of ribeyes and cook the same way to make **Cajun Pan-Fried Beef Sirloin Strips.** I also like to use chopped sirloin steaks and follow the same directions to make **Cajun Pan-Fried Chopped Sirloin Beef Steaks.** (If the chopped sirloin is only ½ pound, cut the seasoning mix down to 1 teaspoon per steak.) Count on about 1,000 calories per serving.

BEEF FLANK STEAK EZORA

1½ pounds of beef flank
steak
1½ tsp. of Beef Seasoning
Mix (see index for recipe)
2 tbsp. of Worcestershire
sauce
½ tsp. of Tabasco sauce
¼ cup of dry red wine
1 tsp. of fresh lemon juice
1 tsp. of sherry
2 tsp. of cornstarch

2 cloves of garlic, minced
3 tbsp. of peanut oil
2 large bell peppers, cut
into strips
1 small onion, cut into
strips
2 tbsp. of minced celery
1 14½-ounce can of stewed
tomatoes
5 large mushrooms, sliced
cooked white rice

Cut the flank steak into thin strips, then season evenly with the Beef Seasoning Mix. Mix the Worcestershire sauce, Tabasco sauce, wine, lemon juice, sherry, and cornstarch; blend well. Put the seasoned steak strips into a large glass bowl, pour the marinade over the steak, and sprinkle the minced garlic over the top of the meat. Let it stand until you are ready to use it.

Heat the oil in a heavy skillet over medium heat until it is hot. Sauté the bell peppers, onions, and celery for 7 minutes until limp and lightly browned. Add the steak strips and marinade and cook over medium heat for about 15 minutes. Add the stewed tomatoes and mix well. Reduce the heat to low, cover partially, and simmer for 30 minutes. The steak and tomatoes should be very tender. Serve hot over cooked white rice. Serves 6 to 8.

Lagniappe: Since this dish is thickened with cornstarch, it will not freeze well. You can refrigerate it after cooking for up to 2 days. To reheat, just bring the dish to a simmer and let the skillet simmer, partially covered, until the meat is hot, about 7 minutes. Without rice, 6 servings have about 282 calories per serving; with ½ cup of cooked white rice, about 394 calories per serving. In 8 servings, count on about 212 calories in each serving without rice or about 324 calories in each serving with rice.

GRILLADES

1 large round steak (heavy
   beef, about 2 to 2½
   pounds)
2 tsp. of Beef Seasoning
   Mix (see index for recipe)
2 tbsp. of cooking oil
2 large onions, chopped
1 small bell pepper,
   chopped
1 tbsp. of chopped celery

1 clove of garlic, minced
1 tsp. of flour
1 cup of Beef Stock (see
   index for recipe) or beef
   broth
1 cup of water
½ tsp. of Tabasco sauce
1 tsp. of Worcestershire
   sauce
cooked white rice

Cut the round steak into serving pieces and season the pieces well with the Beef Seasoning Mix. In a heavy skillet that has a cover, heat the oil over medium heat. Brown the pieces of round steak until they are well browned on both sides. Add the onions, bell pepper, celery, and garlic and sauté them with the meat for 4 minutes. Sprinkle in the flour and blend well.

Add the Beef Stock, reduce the heat to low, cover tightly, and simmer over low heat for 1 hour. Add the water, Tabasco sauce, and Worcestershire sauce and cook for 45 minutes. Serve hot over cooked white rice. Serves 6.

Lagniappe: This recipe may be made completely in advance and either refrigerated or frozen. To reheat, let it thaw in the refrigerator if frozen, then put in a covered skillet and heat until hot over simmering heat. The gravy made in this dish is what is so excellent. The meat is very tender, but the gravy is out of this world. About 450 calories per serving without rice and about 562 calories with ½ cup of cooked white rice.

BEEF À LA MANETTE

1 1¾-pound boneless beef round steak
2½ tsp. of Beef Seasoning Mix (see index for recipe)
3½ tbsp. of peanut oil
1 cup of finely minced carrots
2 medium onions, finely chopped
3 cloves of garlic, minced
1 small bell pepper, finely chopped
1 tbsp. of flour
1 cup of dry burgundy wine

2 cups of Beef Stock (see index for recipe) or beef broth
½ tsp. of Tabasco sauce
1 tbsp. of Worcestershire sauce
½ tsp. of garlic powder
1 tsp. of fresh lemon juice
½ tsp. of freshly ground black pepper
1 bay leaf
½ cup of chopped green onion tops
cooked white rice

Cut the round steak into 2 strips about 3 to 4 inches wide. Then cutting at an angle, cut each strip into thin strips about ½ inch thick and 3 to 4 inches long. Put the steak strips into a mixing bowl and sprinkle the Beef Seasoning Mix on top. Using your fingers, mix the seasoning in with the steak strips evenly.

In the heavy pot, heat the peanut oil until it smokes. Cook the meat a third at a time until all of it is well browned. Set aside for later use. Place the carrots, onions, garlic, and bell pepper in the pot and sauté for 7 minutes, stirring often. Add the flour and cook, stirring constantly, for 5 minutes. It should become somewhat brown, especially where the flour alone touches the bottom of the pan.

Add the wine and blend well (be careful; it will be very hot). Add the Beef Stock, Tabasco sauce, Worcestershire sauce, garlic powder, lemon juice, black pepper, and bay leaf. Add the beef. Reduce the heat to low and cook over low heat just at the simmering point for 45 minutes to 1 hour. Add the green onion tops and serve at once over cooked white rice. Serves 8.

Lagniappe: This dish may be completely made, then either refrigerated or frozen for later use. To reheat, just thaw in the refrigerator if frozen and heat over medium-low heat until the dish is heated through.

Instead of the round steak, you can substitute strips of chuck steak that you have removed most of the fat from. If the chuck steak is not tender, just add a little bit of water and cook it an extra 15 to 30 minutes. About 287 calories per serving without rice and about 399 calories per serving with ½ cup of cooked white rice.

BAKED CHUCK ROAST ABBEVILLE

1 4-pound chuck roast, trimmed of excess fat
4 large cloves of garlic, peeled
½ small bell pepper, cut into strips
1 tbsp. of minced celery
2 green onion bottoms, cut just where the green begins and then cut into fourths

2½ tsp. of Beef Seasoning Mix (see index for recipe)
1 tbsp. of butter, softened
1 tbsp. of Dijon-style mustard
1 tbsp. of Worcestershire sauce
1 cup of dry burgundy wine
½ tsp. of Tabasco sauce

Place the roast on a wooden cutting board. Cut each clove of garlic in half. Using a knife, poke 4 holes about ⅓ of the way down into the top of the roast. Widen the holes by forcing your finger into them. Put in ½ clove of garlic, a strip of bell pepper, a few pieces of celery, and some of the green onion bottoms. Repeat the process until all 4 holes in the top of the roast are stuffed. Turn the roast over and repeat the process on the other side. Sprinkle the roast with the Beef Seasoning Mix, letting some of it fall into the 8 holes, then rub the seasoning into the meat with the palms of your hands.

Preheat the oven to 500 degrees. Mix the butter and mustard until well blended and rub this mixture all over the roast. Place the roast in a roasting pan and bake at 500 degrees for 15 minutes, then reduce the heat to 325 degrees and bake for 2½ to 3 hours or until quite tender.

When the roast is done, remove it from the pan. Add the wine and Tabasco sauce and deglaze the pan over medium heat until all the pan drippings are dissolved. Let the roast cool for 5 minutes before slicing. Serve with the deglazed pan sauce. Serves 12.

Lagniappe: Chuck roast is best eaten right from the oven. It becomes tough and the texture deteriorates as it sets. It also begins to dry out rapidly. If you must refrigerate it, do not slice it until you are ready to serve it. I would not suggest freezing it. About 271 calories per serving of this meat dish.

BEEF LIVER WITH ONIONS

2 tbsp. of olive oil
2 tbsp. of bacon fat
2 medium onions, sliced
and separated into rings
1 pound of beef liver, sliced
about ⅜ inch thick
1½ tsp. of Beef Seasoning
Mix (see index for recipe)

¼ cup of flour
1 tsp. of Beef Seasoning
Mix (see index)
1 tbsp. of fresh lemon juice
1 tsp. of red wine vinegar
¼ cup of dry red wine
½ tsp. of Tabasco sauce

In a heavy skillet over medium heat, heat the olive oil and bacon fat until the oil starts to smoke. Fry the onion rings in the hot oil until they are nicely browned. This will make them sweet and quite tasty. Remove the rings to a warm platter for later use.

Season the liver slices with the 1½ teaspoons of Beef Seasoning Mix, rubbing the seasoning into the liver. Mix the flour and the 1 teaspoon of Beef Seasoning Mix until well blended. Dredge the seasoned liver in the flour mixture until it is coated and shake off the excess. Fry each slice of liver over medium heat in the skillet that you fried the onions in. Cook about 3 minutes on each side or until nicely browned on both sides.

Place the liver on the warm platter and quickly deglaze the skillet with the lemon juice, wine vinegar, wine, and Tabasco sauce. Be sure to dissolve all the pan drippings in the liquid. Return the liver and onions to the skillet and simmer, uncovered, for 2 minutes or until the liver is warm. Serve with plenty of onions and a little of the sauce. Serves 4.

Lagniappe: This is one recipe that you can't prepare in advance. It loses its quality rapidly if you refrigerate or freeze it. Just enjoy it right after it is cooked. You are in for a real treat! A delicious dish for only about 350 calories per serving.

CABBAGE ROLLS

For the rolls:

1 pound of lean ground pork
1 pound of lean ground round
½ pound of ground pork sausage
1½ cups of raw long-grain rice
1 cup of finely chopped onion
2½ cloves of garlic, minced
1 cup of finely minced raw cabbage

½ cup of finely chopped bell pepper
¼ cup of minced celery
¼ cup of minced fresh parsley
3 tsp. of Beef Seasoning Mix (see index for recipe)
½ tsp. of Tabasco sauce
1 tsp. of lemon juice
1 tsp. of Worcestershire sauce
2 large heads of cabbage
water to steam cabbage

For the sauce:

3 tbsp. of bacon grease
1 large onion, chopped
2 stalks of celery, chopped
½ cup of bell pepper, chopped
2 cloves of garlic, minced
1 14½-ounce can of stewed tomatoes
1 15-ounce can of tomato sauce
1 8-ounce can of tomato sauce

1¼ tsp. of Beef Seasoning Mix (see index for recipe)
½ tsp. of Tabasco sauce
2 tbsp. of Worcestershire sauce
1 bay leaf
½ tsp. of sweet basil
¼ tsp. of freshly ground black pepper
water to cover cabbage rolls

To make the rolls:

In a large mixing bowl, mix the ground pork, ground round, ground sausage, rice, the cup of finely chopped onion, the 2½ minced cloves of garlic, the minced cabbage, the finely chopped bell pepper, the minced celery, parsley, the 3 teaspoons of Beef Seasoning Mix, ½ teaspoon of Tabasco sauce, lemon juice, and the teaspoon of Worcestershire Sauce until thoroughly mixed. Set aside.

Remove the outer leaves from the cabbage and cut the core out carefully. Run your tap water on hot until it is as hot as it will get, then let the water run into the hole in the cabbage to loosen the leaves. Peel the leaves off one at a time and place them in a steamer or a large pan of boiling water. Steam or boil until the leaves are limp and easy to bend. Fill a leaf, stem part toward you, with a heaping tablespoon of the meat-rice mixture. Roll the leaf away from you and secure the roll with toothpicks. Place the roll in a large dutch oven or saucepan with a lid. Repeat the process until all the mixture is used.

To make the sauce:

In a large saucepan over medium heat, melt the bacon grease. Sauté the chopped onion, the chopped celery, the chopped bell pepper, and the 2 minced cloves of garlic until they begin to brown on the edges, about 7 minutes. Add the tomato pieces from the stewed tomatoes and sauté for 3 more minutes. Then add the liquid from the stewed tomatoes can and the tomato sauce. Cook for 5 minutes over medium heat, then add the 1¼ teaspoons of Beef Seasoning Mix, ½ teaspoon of Tabasco sauce, the 2 tablespoons of Worcestershire sauce, bay leaf, sweet basil, and black pepper. Cook the sauce for 10 more minutes at a simmer.

Pour the sauce over the cabbage leaves and fill the pot to just above the cabbage rolls with water. Simmer over low heat for about 1½ hours or until the rice is tender. Serve hot. Serves 12.

Lagniappe: This is a great make-ahead dish. You can completely cook it and either freeze or refrigerate it, or freeze all your leftovers for a great meal at a later date. I suggest freezing it in individual portions with a little of the sauce around. It really freezes well and is easy to handle.

To reheat, just thaw in the refrigerator or microwave if frozen and bake at 350 degrees for about 12 to 15 minutes. The rolls brown nicely around the edges and look great. You can also just take them right from the freezer and thaw them in the microwave for 5 minutes, then heat at 80 percent power for 3 minutes. About 445 calories per serving of this excellent dish.

CAJUN MEATLOAF

2 pounds of ground chuck
1½ tsp. of Beef Seasoning
   Mix (see index for recipe)
1 onion, finely chopped
2 cloves of garlic, minced
3 tbsp. of minced celery
¼ cup of finely chopped
   bell pepper
¼ cup of minced fresh
   parsley
¼ cup of green onion tops
1 cup of diced French bread
¼ tsp. of Tabasco sauce

1 tbsp. of Worcestershire
   sauce
2 large eggs, well beaten
1 tsp. of fresh lemon juice
1 tbsp. of bacon fat
½ cup of finely minced
   onion
1 tbsp. of minced bell
   pepper
¼ tsp. of Tabasco sauce
1 14½-ounce can of stewed
   tomatoes
¼ tsp. of sweet basil

Preheat the oven to 275 degrees. Mix together in a large mixing bowl the ground chuck, Beef Seasoning Mix, the finely chopped onion, 1 minced clove of garlic, 2 tablespoons of minced celery, the ¼ cup of bell pepper, parsley, green onion tops, French bread, ¼ teaspoon of Tabasco sauce, Worcestershire sauce, eggs, and lemon juice. When well mixed, shape in a loaf pan. Bake at 275 degrees for 2 hours.

While the meatloaf is baking, melt the bacon fat over medium heat in a saucepan. Sauté the ½ cup of onion, the remaining garlic clove, the remaining tablespoon of minced celery, and the tablespoon of bell pepper for 5 minutes, then add the remaining ¼ teaspoon of Tabasco sauce, stewed tomatoes, and sweet basil. Simmer over very low heat for about 45 minutes. When the meatloaf is baked, remove from the oven and spread the tomato mixture on top. Return the meatloaf to the oven and continue cooking for 30 to 45 more minutes. Remove from the oven and let it cool somewhat before slicing it. Serve warm. Serves 8.

Lagniappe: This is an easy recipe. The only thing hard about it is the long cooking time, but the end result makes it worth it. The loaf will be very juicy and tender. You can bake it completely and refrigerate it, or freeze the whole loaf (or parts of it) for later use. Thaw at room temperature if frozen and reheat in a warm oven. About 333 calories per serving of this dish.

MEATLOAF ANDRE BRUN

1½ pounds of ground chuck
½ pound of pork sausage
1 onion, finely chopped
1 stalk of celery, finely chopped
¼ cup of finely chopped bell pepper
2 cloves of garlic, minced
8 large mushrooms, sliced
1 cup of diced French bread
¼ cup of evaporated milk

½ cup of stewed tomatoes
1½ tsp. of Beef Seasoning Mix (see index for recipe)
½ tsp. of Tabasco sauce
1 tsp. of Worcestershire sauce
1 large egg, beaten
¼ cup of minced fresh parsley
¼ cup of minced green onion tops

Preheat the oven to 350 degrees. In a large mixing bowl, mix all ingredients together until well mixed. Form mixture into a loaf pan, shaping the loaf nicely. Cut a slit with a knife about 1 inch deep along the entire top of the meatloaf, then cut about 3 slits across the long slit. Bake for about 1½ hours or until the meatloaf is nicely browned. Let it cool for 5 minutes before slicing and serving. Serves 8.

Lagniappe: This dish may be made completely in advance and either stored in the refrigerator for use later in the day or frozen for later use. To reheat, let it thaw in the refrigerator if frozen and heat in the oven at 350 degrees for 12 to 15 minutes. Remove and let cool for 3 to 5 minutes, then slice it or remove it whole to a platter for slicing. About 391 calories per serving.

STUFFED TURNIPS MANETTE

8 large, tender turnips
water to steam turnips
1 pound of ground chuck
1¼ pounds of ground
 pan sausage (any spicy
 group sausage)
1 large yellow onion,
 chopped
1 cup of chopped bell
 pepper
2 stalks of celery, chopped
4 cloves of garlic, minced
3 tsp. of Beef Seasoning
 Mix (see index for recipe)

½ tsp. of Tabasco sauce
½ tsp. of garlic powder
1 tbsp. of Worcestershire
 sauce
1½ cups of cooked white
 rice
1 cup of bread crumbs
1 cup of finely chopped
 green onions
¼ cup of minced fresh
 parsley
¼ cup of bread crumbs

Wash the turnips. Cut off the greens and the roots. Scrub lightly to remove all dirt from the outside. Place the turnips in a steamer and steam for 15 minutes once the water begins to boil.

While the turnips are steaming, brown the ground chuck and pan sausage in a large, heavy pot over medium heat until all the meat has turned from red to brown. Add the onion, bell pepper, celery, and garlic and sauté for 5 minutes. Season with Beef Seasoning Mix, Tabasco sauce, garlic powder, and Worcestershire sauce, and remove from the heat.

When the turnips are through steaming and are cool enough to handle, scoop out the center and inside of each turnip, leaving about ½ inch of turnip all around the inside. Chop the turnip pulp that you have removed into medium-fine pieces and add it to the meat mixture.

Return the meat-turnip mixture to medium heat and cook for about 7 minutes, stirring constantly. Add the rice and the cup of bread crumbs and mix in well. Cook for 2 minutes, then add the green onion and parsley. Mix in well, then use this mixture to stuff the turnip shells, packing in as much mixture as possible. Sprinkle the tops of the turnips with the ¼ cup of bread crumbs and bake at 350 degrees for 30 minutes. Serve hot. Serves 8.

Lagniappe: This is a really great make-ahead dish. You can prepare the dish up to the baking and freeze or refrigerate. To heat, just defrost in the refrigerator if frozen, then bake as above.

As a variation, if the turnip shells do not look good, you can just fill an au gratin dish with the mixture, bake, and serve. This is a great main dish or a nice side dish with any meat or seafood. This very generous serving size has only about 544 calories. To reduce the calories to about 380 per serving, just cut the sausage down to ½ pound and the bread crumbs that are added to the mixture down to ½ cup and proceed as above. The taste will still be excellent.

RICE DRESSING
(DIRTY RICE)

2 pounds of ground pork
1 pound of ground beef
2 pounds of mixture of chicken giblets, livers, and hearts, finely ground
¼ cup of peanut oil
2 large onions, finely chopped
1 cup of finely chopped celery
2 medium bell peppers, finely chopped

2½ tbsp. of dark roux (see index for recipe)
1¾ cups of Chicken Stock (see index for recipe) or chicken broth
½ tsp. of Tabasco sauce
salt and black pepper to taste
1 cup of chopped green onion
3 cups of cooked white rice

In a large, heavy pot, brown the pork, beef, and giblet mixture in the peanut oil over medium heat. When well browned, add the onions, celery, and bell peppers to the meat mixture. Cook over medium-low heat, stirring often, for 30 minutes. Add the roux and

Chicken Stock and blend until the roux has dissolved. Season with Tabasco sauce, salt, and black pepper. Simmer for 1 hour. When the hour is up, add the green onion and rice. Blend well and serve at once. Serves 10 to 12.

Lagniappe: Dirty rice is a Cajun tradition. The name comes from the fact that the rice is colored from the meats. Don't let the name turn you off; try it once and you'll eat it no matter what it's called! This dressing can also be used to stuff a turkey.

It can be made in advance and either refrigerated or frozen for later use. The dressing does not lose any quality with this treatment. To reheat, defrost in the refrigerator if frozen and heat in the top of a double boiler, bake in the oven, or—better yet—reheat in the microwave. In the double boiler, you will have to stir the dressing a number of times to keep it from sticking. To bake it, cover it tightly with foil and bake at 300 degrees for about 15 minutes. In the microwave, cover with plastic wrap, punch a few holes in the top of the wrap with a fork, and heat at about 80 percent power for about 5 minutes.

In 10 servings, count on around 603 calories; in 12 servings, about 503. No change recommended.

This recipe is from Rose LeBlanc, my mother-in-law.

HOG HEAD CHEESE

1 fresh picnic ham (3½ to
4 pounds)
4 fresh ham hocks
6 fresh pigs' feet
3 stalks of celery
1 carrot
1 bunch of fresh parsley,
cleaned, half of it minced
1 small onion, sliced into
fourths
1½ gallons of water
12 whole black peppercorns
2 whole bay leaves
2 tbsp. of salt
½ tsp. of thyme

8 green onions, finely
chopped
¼ cup of chopped bell
pepper
2 tbsp. of Worcestershire
sauce
¾ tsp. of Tabasco sauce
½ tsp. of garlic powder
½ tsp. of onion powder
¼ tsp. of white pepper
¼ cup of minced celery
½ tsp. of sweet basil
salt to taste
4 envelopes of unflavored
gelatine
1 cup of hot water

In a very large pot or gumbo pot, put the picnic ham, ham hocks, pigs' feet, stalks of celery, carrot, the whole parsley, and onion. Cover with the 1½ gallons of water. Add the peppercorns, bay leaves, salt, and thyme and bring to a boil over high heat. When the liquid begins to boil, reduce heat to low, cover, and simmer for about 4 hours or until the meat falls off the bones and is very tender.

Let it cool, then strain the liquid from the meat and vegetables. Let the liquid stand and cool. Pull the meat from the bones and separate the meat from the fat. Grind the good pieces of meat in a meat grinder. Also grind the carrot and 1 stalk of celery. Set the meat aside for later use.

Skim all the excess fat from the top of the liquid that you set aside to cool. Put the meat back into the liquid and add the green onions, minced parsley, bell pepper, Worcestershire sauce, Tabasco sauce, garlic powder, onion powder, white pepper, minced celery, and sweet basil. Mix well. Taste for desired amount of salt and add more if needed.

Add the unflavored gelatine to the cup of hot water and stir until it is dissolved. Add this to the meat mixture and stir well. Pour the mixture into a shallow casserole dish or baking pan. Refrigerate until firm. Cut into squares and serve chilled. Serves 12.

Lagniappe: You can make this well in advance and chill it in the refrigerator for 3 to 4 days, or you can make it up to the point of adding the gelatine, then freeze for much later use. When you are ready to use it, simply heat the mixture to the boiling point and remove it from the heat. Add the gelatine mixture, pour it into the pan, and refrigerate it until it is firm. Cut and serve. This is excellent for a light lunch, a snack, or an appetizer. It also makes excellent party food. About 646 calories per serving.

You might notice that this recipe does not call for a real hog's head. The cheese was originally made with a hog's head instead of other hog parts, but today hog heads are not so readily available. (In the Louisiana countryside, though, it is still often made with the real thing.) This recipe is just as exceptional, and you don't have to have two eyes staring at you when you uncover the pot!

TENDERLOIN OF PORK FLORENTINE

1 pork tenderloin (about 1 pound)
2 tsp. of Pork Seasoning Mix (see index for recipe)
6 tbsp. of unsalted butter
2 cloves of garlic, minced
1 pound of fresh spinach, cleaned and very finely minced
½ cup of finely minced fresh parsley
2 green onions, finely minced

1 tsp. of Pork Seasoning Mix (see index)
½ tsp. of Tabasco sauce
2 tbsp. of seasoned bread crumbs
2 eggs, beaten
½ cup of seasoned bread crumbs
½ tsp. of Pork Seasoning Mix (see index)
3 tbsp. of peanut oil

Cut the tenderloin into four equal circles, then cut a slit in each circle about ⅔ of the way through. Spread each piece of meat out from the slit with your hands and pound the meat out into large thin pieces with a kitchen mallet. The meat should be about ¼ inch thick. Repeat until all 4 are done. Season each tenderloin on both sides with the 2 teaspoons of Pork Seasoning Mix, then set them aside for later use.

In a saucepan over medium heat, melt 3 tablespoons of butter. Sauté the garlic, spinach, parsley, and green onions for 7 minutes, stirring constantly. Add the teaspoon of Pork Seasoning Mix and the Tabasco sauce and cook for 2 minutes. Divide the mixture in half, leaving half in the saucepan over very low heat. Put the other half into a mixing bowl and mix in the 2 tablespoons of seasoned bread crumbs; mix until very well blended. Spoon one-fourth of the mixture onto the center of a flattened tenderloin and fold the edges together and press well with your hands until all the sides are sealed. Repeat until all 4 are done.

Dip each of the stuffed tenderloins into the beaten eggs. Mix the ½ cup of seasoned bread crumbs with the remaining ½ teaspoon of Pork Seasoning Mix. Dip each stuffed tenderloin into the bread crumb mixture and set it on a plate. In a large skillet, heat the peanut oil over medium heat until it is hot. Add the remaining 3 tablespoons of butter, then add the stuffed pork tenderloins one at a time. Sauté them well on both sides until they are golden brown and cooked through, about 10 to 12 minutes. Drain on paper towels and serve hot with some of the spinach mixture that was left warming on the stove. Serves 4.

Lagniappe: This is very elegant and not difficult to do. You can prepare the tenderloins all the way to dipping them into the bread crumb mixture, then cover and refrigerate them for up to a day before you cook them. Do not freeze or try to reheat them after they are cooked. Count on about 695 calories per serving of this main-dish meat.

QUICK PORK CASSEROLE

2½ pounds of pork steaks
2 tsp. of Pork Seasoning
  Mix (see index for recipe)
1 16-ounce package of
  spinach noodles
1 tbsp. of butter
1 large onion, chopped
1 medium bell pepper, cut
  into thin slices
1 stalk of celery, minced
2 cloves of garlic, minced
12 large mushrooms, sliced
1 17-ounce can very young
  small early peas

1 10¾-ounce can cream of
  mushroom soup
1 10¾-ounce can cream of
  chicken soup
¼ cup of diced pimento
½ pound of grated Swiss
  cheese
1 pound of grated sharp
  cheddar cheese
¼ cup of bread crumbs
butter to grease casserole
  dish

Season the pork steaks well with the Pork Seasoning Mix. Bake for 30 minutes at 375 degrees, turning the steaks once while baking. Remove and let cool. Cook the spinach noodles according to the directions on the package and drain.

In a large, heavy saucepan over medium heat, melt the butter, then sauté the onions, bell pepper, celery, and garlic until the onions are limp and clear, about 5 minutes. Add the mushrooms and sauté for 3 minutes. Remove from the heat and let the pan cool.

Pick the meat off the cool pork steaks, taking care to avoid the fat. Chop the meat into small pieces. Put the meat into the saucepan and blend well. Add the cooked noodles and blend them well with the meat and vegetables. Add the peas, mushroom soup, chicken soup, pimento, and Swiss cheese and carefully mix together.

Pour into a lightly greased 2½- to 3-quart casserole dish and cover with the cheddar cheese, then sprinkle the top with the bread crumbs. Bake for 20 to 25 minutes at 350 degrees. Serve at once. Serves 8.

Lagniappe: This is a great make-ahead dish. You can bake this dish completely, then refrigerate or freeze it for later use. It also does well if you put it into individual baking dishes instead of the casserole dish, top each dish with cheddar cheese and bread crumbs, and freeze the individual dishes. To reheat, just thaw in the refrigerator and bake at 300 degrees until hot, about 15 minutes.

It is also a very versatile dish. You can use 2½ cups of chopped cooked turkey instead of the pork and follow the recipe as given (without the cooking of the pork) to make **Quick Turkey Casserole.** You can do the same by using 2½ cups of chopped cooked chicken to make **Quick Chicken Casserole.** You can even use 1¼ pounds of boiled shrimp as the pork substitute to make an excellent **Quick Shrimp Casserole.** Bon appétit!

The pork version has about 1,061 calories per serving; the turkey version, about 769; the chicken version, about 760; and the shrimp version about 725. (These are very generous servings.)

CAJUN PAN-FRIED PORK CHOPS

4 large center-cut pork chops, ½ inch thick

4 tsp. of Pork Seasoning Mix (see index for recipe)
3 tbsp. of peanut oil

Season the pork chops well with 1 teaspoon of Pork Seasoning Mix each, pushing the seasoning mix into the meat with the palms of your hands.

In a heavy black iron pot over high heat, heat the peanut oil until it begins to smoke. Be sure to have your stove hood fan on full power, because this will smoke up quite a lot. Place 2 chops in the pan, one at a time, and cook over high heat for 3 minutes on each side, sliding them around a little in the pan to prevent sticking. (Don't worry about the color of the cooked chops; they will be quite black, but they will taste heavenly.)

Place the cooked chops on a warm plate, cover with aluminum

foil, and keep warm in a 190-degree oven until the other chops are cooked. Serve hot as soon as the last 2 chops are cooked. Serves 4.

Lagniappe: This is a great dish, but there is not anything you can do to it in advance. Its cooking time is not that long, so you won't have a lot of waiting to do. It does smoke up your kitchen quite a lot, so be sure that your exhaust fan is in good working order. My grandma used to make this in the kitchen with all the windows open. The odor left the kitchen in a short time, but it smelled good for miles around! About 495 calories per serving of this dish.

STUFFED PORK CHOPS DE LAUSSAT

4 large pork chops, 1¼ inches thick
2 tsp. of Pork Seasoning Mix (see index for recipe)
3 strips of bacon, chopped
1 medium onion, chopped
2 tbsp. of chopped green pepper
2 tbsp. of chopped celery
1 clove of garlic, minced
2 cups of diced fresh French bread

½ tsp. of Chicken Seasoning Mix (see index for recipe)
1 egg, well beaten
2 tbsp. of milk
¼ tsp. of Tabasco sauce
½ cup of flour
1½ tbsp. of peanut oil
1 stalk of celery, julienned
1 onion, julienned
4 tender carrots, julienned
1½ cups of Beef Stock (see index for recipe) or beef broth

Preheat the oven to 375 degrees. Season each of the pork chops equally with 1 teaspoon of Pork Seasoning Mix. Cut a slit to make a pocket in each of the pork chops that is large enough to hold about ½ cup of the stuffing.

In a large, heavy skillet, sauté the bacon until it is brown and crisp. Add the onion, green pepper, celery, and garlic. Sauté for 4 minutes over medium heat. Add the French bread and sauté for 3 minutes; the bread should brown somewhat. Add the Chicken Seasoning Mix, egg, milk, and Tabasco sauce and mix well until it is all blended together.

In a large mixing bowl, mix the flour and the other teaspoon of Pork Seasoning Mix until well blended. Stuff one-fourth of the stuffing mix into the slit in each pork chop. Coat each stuffed chop well with the seasoned flour. Clean the skillet you used earlier and heat the peanut oil to medium-high. Brown the stuffed chops well on both sides and set them aside. Add the julienned vegetables and sauté for 2 minutes. Remove and drain.

Place the vegetables in the bottom of a baking pan and place the chops on top of the vegetables. Bake for 20 minutes at 375 degrees and remove from the oven. Reduce the oven temperature to 250 degrees. Add the Beef Stock to the pan and return the pan to the oven. Bake for 1 hour and 15 minutes at 250 degrees. Serve hot with pan drippings and vegetables. Serves 4.

Lagniappe: This dish may be made in advance through the first baking. Add the beef stock, then cover and refrigerate. When ready to use, bake for 1 hour and 20 minutes. I would not recommend freezing this dish. Count on around 725 calories per serving. The only way to cut calories here is to eat half a chop!

BOUDIN LEBLANC

5 pounds of fresh pork
  shoulder
2 pounds of pork liver
water to cover meat
2 tsp. of salt
2 large onions, chopped
4 cloves of garlic, crushed
salt to taste

1 tsp. of red pepper
1 tsp. of black pepper
8 cups of cooked short-grain
  white rice
1 package sausage casings
1 gallon of simmering water
1 tsp. of salt
1 tsp. of Tabasco sauce

Put the pork shoulder and pork liver in a large stockpot and cover with cold water. Bring to a boil over high heat, then reduce the heat to simmer. Add the 2 teaspoons of salt, the onions, and the garlic, cover, and simmer for 3 hours.

Remove the meat from the stockpot, reserving the liquid for later use. When the meat is cool, debone the pork shoulder. Grind the shoulder meat and liver together and season the meat with the salt to taste, red pepper, and black pepper. Mix the meat and rice together; if it is too dry, add enough reserved stock liquid to moisten the mixture well.

Stuff the mixture into the sausage casings and tie a knot in the casings at intervals of a foot or so. Put the gallon of simmering water in another large stockpot and add the 1 teaspoon of salt and Tabasco sauce. As you finish stuffing the boudin into the casings and tying it (be sure to tie both ends), put it into the warm water to "uniform" it throughout the casings. Serve hot. You can also fry the boudin in a small amount of bacon fat or butter until it is warmed through. Serves 10 to 12.

Lagniappe: As per the directions, this is a dish that is made in abundance. You can serve it right from the simmering pot, refrigerate it for up to 4 days, or freeze it (it freezes well in plastic Ziploc bags, but try to keep air out of the bags if possible). Be sure to put the date on the bag so you can use the oldest packages from the freezer first.

To make **Blood Boudin** or **Red Boudin,** you must mix fresh pork blood with the rice and meat as you mix the sausage stuffing together. I would not advise this unless you have just butchered a whole pig and you are sure the blood is fresh and free of bacteria. Remember, blood is a medium for growing all kinds of bacteria, so you should take extreme care. I would not suggest refrigerating or freezing blood boudin. If you make it, be sure to eat it right away. Blood boudin is a favorite Cajun dish, but you almost have to be a true Cajun to eat it!

In 10 servings, there are about 831 calories each, and in 12, count on 693 calories per serving. No way to cut down on calories and have boudin too!

This recipe is from Rose LeBlanc, my mother-in-law.

PORK JAMBALAYA DON LOUIS

2 pounds of center-cut pork
  chops
2 tbsp. of peanut oil
2 cups of baked ham, diced
  in ½-inch pieces
1½ tbsp. of unsalted butter
2 medium onions, chopped
2 cups of whole tomatoes,
  chopped
2 cloves of garlic, minced
2 stalks of celery, minced
1 medium bell pepper,
  chopped
3 tbsp. of minced turnip

2 cups of uncooked white
  rice
3 cups of Chicken Stock
  (see index for recipe) or
  chicken broth
1 cup of water
1½ tsp. of Pork Seasoning
  Mix (see index for recipe)
½ tsp. of Tabasco sauce
2 tbsp. of Worcestershire
  sauce
¼ cup of minced fresh
  parsley
¼ cup of finely chopped
  green onion tops

In a large, heavy iron skillet that has a cover, fry the pork chops over medium heat in the peanut oil. When the meat is well browned on both sides, take it out of the skillet and set it aside. Add the ham and fry it for 5 minutes, stirring constantly. Remove it and set it aside for later use.

Melt the butter in the skillet and add the onions. Sauté for 4 minutes, then add the chopped tomatoes, garlic, celery, bell pepper, and turnip and sauté for 7 minutes, stirring constantly. Add the rice and sauté for 4 minutes. Return the chops and ham to the skillet and mix with the rice. Add the Chicken Stock and water and stir through. Add the Pork Seasoning Mix and raise the heat to high. Bring the mixture to a hard boil, then reduce the heat to low, cover, and simmer for 15 minutes.

Remove the cover, stir well to be sure nothing is sticking to the bottom, and continue cooking, uncovered, for 45 minutes, stirring 2 or 3 times. When the liquid is absorbed and the rice is tender, add the Tabasco sauce, Worcestershire sauce, parsley, and green onion tops. Serve hot. Serves 6 to 8.

Lagniappe: This dish may be made in advance and refrigerated or frozen. To reheat, just thaw in the refrigerator if frozen, then place the dish in a heavy skillet, add ¼ cup of water, and cook over low heat until the dish is heated through, about 20 minutes. Be sure to stir constantly. This excellent dish is basically a one-dish meal. Six servings have about 677 calories per serving, and 8 servings have about 508 calories each serving.

PORK CHOPS DE SAUVOLLE

6 large pork chops, cut 1
  inch thick
1½ tsp. of Pork Seasoning
  Mix (see index for the
  recipe)
butter to grease baking dish
1 large onion, chopped
1 stalk of celery, chopped
2 cloves of garlic, minced
1 small bell pepper,
  chopped

3 small tomatoes, skinned
  and chopped
¼ tsp. of Tabasco sauce
½ tsp. of salt
½ tsp. of sugar
1 bay leaf, crushed
¼ tsp. of black pepper
1 tsp. of Worcestershire
  sauce
1 tsp. of lemon juice
1 tbsp. of white wine
cooked white rice

Preheat the oven to 350 degrees. Season the chops equally with the Pork Seasoning Mix on both sides. In a large, heavy skillet over medium heat, fry the chops until they are browned on both sides. They should give up enough fat to allow you to continue with the remaining sautéing. Remove the chops to a greased baking dish.

Add the onions, celery, garlic, and bell pepper to the skillet and sauté for 4 minutes until limp and clear. Add the tomatoes and sauté for 3 minutes. Add the Tabasco sauce, salt, sugar, bay leaf, black pepper, Worcestershire sauce, lemon juice, and wine. Cover, reduce the heat to low, and simmer for 10 minutes. Pour this sauce over the pork chops in the baking dish. Bake at 350 degrees for 45 minutes or until the chops are tender. Serve hot with cooked white rice. Serves 6.

Lagniappe: This dish may be made in advance and refrigerated or frozen. If you freeze it, cook it completely and freeze. When ready to use, thaw it in the refrigerator and bake at 350 degrees, partially covered, until hot, about 10 to 12 minutes. If you want to make it in advance for use later in the day, do not bake it. Just brown the chops, make the sauce, and cover the chops with the sauce, then cover the baking dish tightly with plastic wrap or aluminum foil and refrigerate until you are ready to bake.

You can use this same recipe with chicken if you like. The only thing you do differently is fry the chicken in 3 tablespoons of bacon fat; the rest of the recipe is the same.

There are about 577 calories per serving without rice and about 690 calories per serving with ½ cup of cooked white rice. The only way to cut calories here is to use ½-inch-thick chops. This will cut the calories down to about 400 per serving without rice and about 512 with rice.

HAM LOAF

3 strips of bacon, chopped
1 clove of garlic, minced
½ cup of finely chopped
  onion
¼ cup of finely chopped
  bell pepper
¼ cup of finely chopped
  celery
6 large eggs
¾ cup of milk
1½ cups of flour
2½ tsp. of baking powder
½ tsp. of baking soda
½ tsp. of salt

½ tsp. of Tabasco sauce
¼ tsp. of sweet basil
1 tbsp. of minced fresh
  parsley
¼ pound of Swiss cheese,
  cut into small cubes
¼ pound of sharp cheddar
  cheese, cut into small
  cubes
1½ cups of cooked ham,
  cut into small cubes
butter and flour to grease
  and flour loaf pan

In a saucepan, fry the bacon over medium heat until it is brown and crisp. Add the garlic, onion, bell pepper, and celery and sauté for 4 minutes. Remove from the heat and let cool.

Beat the eggs at high speed until they begin to foam. Add the milk, flour, baking powder, baking soda, salt, and Tabasco sauce and beat until smooth. Add the bacon-vegetable mixture (including the bacon grease) and beat well. Stir in the remaining ingredients until well mixed. Pour into a greased and floured 9 by 5 by 3 loaf pan and bake at 350 degrees for 45 to 55 minutes or until a toothpick inserted in the center comes out clean and the top is nicely browned. Serve hot. Serves 6 to 8.

Lagniappe: You can bake this completely and freeze it for later use. Just thaw it in the refrigerator until defrosted, then heat in the oven at 300 degrees until the loaf is warm. This is excellent with just a salad on the side. In 6 servings, count on around 482 calories per serving; in 8 servings, count on about 362 calories per serving.

SAUSAGE JAMBALAYA TELLIER

2 pounds of pork smoked sausage, sliced 1 inch thick

2 tbsp. of peanut oil

2 medium onions, finely chopped

4 cloves of garlic, minced

2 stalks of celery, minced

1 medium bell pepper, finely chopped

2 tbsp. of minced carrot

2 cups of uncooked white rice

3 cups of Beef Stock (see index for recipe) or beef broth

1 cup of water

2 tbsp. of red wine

1½ tsp. of Pork Seasoning Mix (see index for recipe)

¼ cup of minced fresh parsley

¼ cup of finely chopped green onion

½ tsp. of Tabasco sauce

1 tbsp. of Worcestershire sauce

In a large, heavy iron skillet, fry the sausage in the peanut oil over medium heat until it is well browned, about 15 minutes. Add the onions, garlic, celery, bell pepper, and carrot and cook until the vegetables are wilted, about 4 minutes. Reduce the heat to low;

cover the dish and cook for 10 minutes. Add the rice and sauté it for 5 minutes or until it is nicely browned.

Add the Beef Stock, water, and wine and bring the dish to a boil over medium heat. When it comes to a full boil, reduce the heat to low and simmer very slowly until the rice is tender, about 1 hour. When the liquid is almost completely gone, add the Pork Seasoning Mix, parsley, green onion, Tabasco sauce, and Worcestershire sauce. Serve hot. Serves 6.

Lagniappe: This is a great make-ahead dish. You can either refrigerate it for up to 4 days or freeze it; this even seems to improve the dish. To reheat, thaw in the refrigerator if frozen and return to a large iron skillet. Add about ¼ cup of water and cook over a low fire, covered, for about 10 minutes. Remove the cover, raise the heat to medium, and cook for 7 more minutes, stirring constantly to prevent the jambalaya from sticking.

This is the dish that we almost always eat on Christmas Eve and any other time we feel like a hearty dish. About 590 calories per serving; you can't really cut down on the calorie count because the main ingredient, sausage, is where the bulk of the calories comes from.

CARAMEL SAUSAGE

3½ pounds of pork smoked sausage, sliced ½ inch thick
1 stick of unsalted butter
1½ cups of dark brown sugar, packed

1½ cups of light brown sugar, packed
1 cup of white vinegar
½ cup of dry burgundy wine
½ tsp. of Tabasco sauce
1 small onion, sliced

In a large skillet with a lid, fry the sausage over high heat, stirring often to brown it and removing some of the fat as it cooks. As the pieces brown, remove them from the skillet and set them aside for later use.

Clean the skillet and return it to the stove over medium-low heat. Add the butter and let it completely melt. When it is melted, add the dark and light brown sugar. Stir it in until it begins to dissolve in the butter, then cook for 5 minutes. Remove from the heat and add the vinegar, but be careful, because it will splatter and let off a lot of steam. Add the wine, return the skillet to the stove, and cook, stirring constantly, until the mixture becomes a brown sauce with all the sugar dissolved.

Add the Tabasco sauce and onion and mix well. Add the browned sausage to the skillet, reduce the heat to low, and cover. Let the sausage simmer in the caramel sauce for 20 minutes. Serve hot. Serves 8.

Lagniappe: This can be completely made in advance and either refrigerated or frozen for later use. You can serve this as a main dish as you would barbecued sausage (with plenty of caramel sauce) or as an appetizer with toothpicks. You can let it stay on a warming tray or in a chafing dish for a few hours if serving it as an appetizer. To reheat, just thaw in the refrigerator if frozen and heat in a skillet or saucepan over low heat until the sausage is heated through.

For a little variety, add 1 can of pineapple chunks and 1 medium bell pepper cut into strips to the dish. You will find that not only the sausage will be eaten, but also the pineapple, onion, and bell pepper. Loaded with about 1,036 calories per serving, but it tastes like even more!

CAJUN PAN-FRIED VEAL SIRLOIN STEAK

2 white veal sirloin
    steaks, about 1 pound
    each

4 tsp. of Veal Seasoning
    Mix (see index for recipe)
3 tbsp. of peanut oil

Season the steaks well with the Veal Seasoning Mix, pushing the seasoning into the steaks with the palms of your hands. Heat the peanut oil in a heavy black iron pot over medium-high heat until the oil starts to smoke. Fry the first veal steak for 1 minute on each side, then remove it to a warm plate, cover it with aluminum foil, and keep it warm in a 175-degree oven until the other steak is cooked.

Repeat the process for the other steak. (The black coating on the veal is just the seasonings that have charred.) Cut each steak in half and serve at once. Serves 4.

Lagniappe: This cannot be made in advance. The cooking time is so short that you don't have any need to prepare it in advance, anyhow. Keep your stove hood fan on high, for this will smoke up your kitchen. About 435 calories per serving of this meat dish.

VEAL DE RIDDER

2 white veal round steaks (1 pound each with bone)
3 tsp. of Veal Seasoning Mix (see index for recipe)
½ cup of flour
¼ cup of peanut oil

½ stick of unsalted butter
2 cups of Crabmeat Dressing (see index for recipe)
½ cup of Hollandaise Sauce (see index for recipe)

Cut each veal round steak in half. Remove the bone and cut off any excess fat. Using a metal kitchen mallet, pound the 4 veal cutlets well on both sides until they are about one-third as thick as they were when you started. Season the cutlets with 2 teaspoons of the Veal Seasoning Mix.

Mix the flour and the other teaspoon of Veal Seasoning Mix in a large mixing bowl. Coat each cutlet evenly and completely with the flour mixture, shaking off any excess. Heat the peanut oil over medium heat in a heavy skillet. When the oil is very hot, add the unsalted butter and stir until it is melted. Add the cutlets one at a time and sauté them for 2 minutes on each side. Place them on a paper towel to drain, then place them on a heated plate and keep them warm in a 200-degree oven until all 4 are cooked.

When ready to serve, place ½ cup of the Crabmeat Dressing on top of each cutlet and cover the dressing with ⅛ cup of Hollandaise Sauce. Serve at once. Serves 4.

Lagniappe: This dish may not be made in advance. You can, however, pound the steaks in advance so you will save some time in later preparation. Forget about counting calories with this dish—your counter won't go this high! About 805 calories per serving.

ROAST LEG OF LAMB

1 leg of young lamb (about
    4½ to 5 pounds)
3 cloves of garlic, peeled
¼ small bell pepper,
    cleaned
½ stalk of celery
¼ cayenne pepper or other
    red pepper
juice of 2 large lemons
1 tbsp. of olive oil
2½ tsp. of Veal Seasoning
    Mix (see index for recipe)

1 tsp. of freshly ground
    black pepper
3 tbsp. of unsalted butter,
    softened
½ cup of burgundy wine
½ tsp. of Tabasco sauce
1½ tbsp. of Worcestershire
    sauce
juice of 1 lemon
juice of ½ lime
¼ cup of water
½ stick of butter, cut into
    small pieces

Trim the leg of lamb of excess fat. Chop the garlic, bell pepper, celery, and cayenne pepper into small pieces to stuff into the lamb leg. Make holes in the meat with a large knife and force some of the vegetable pieces into the holes with your finger. Repeat until all the vegetable pieces are used.

Rub the juice from the 2 large lemons all over the leg, taking care to place a dish under the leg to catch the excess juice as it drips off. Cover the leg with plastic wrap and refrigerate for 1 hour. Remove and rub with the juice again, then rub the leg with the olive oil using your hands, covering all parts of the leg. Sprinkle with the Veal Seasoning Mix, then rub the black pepper into the meat. Using your hands, rub the softened butter all over the meat.

Place the leg on a wire rack inside a baking dish large enough to hold it. Bake at 275 degrees for 1½ to 2 hours or until the meat is done to your liking. Remove the leg from the pan and remove all of the grease from the pan drippings with a spoon or a bulb baster. Deglaze the drippings by adding the wine, Tabasco sauce, Worcestershire sauce, lemon juice, lime juice, and water. Heat over medium heat until all the drippings are dissolved.

Remove from the heat and whip in the butter pieces until they are dissolved. Serve the lamb warm with the deglazed sauce on the side or with Béarnaise sauce or mint sauce. Serves 8 to 10.

Lagniappe: This should be eaten right after it is cooked. The meat will be at its best then and should not be cooked in advance. You can stuff and butter it up to 2 days in advance and store it in the refrigerator. In 8 servings, count on about 614 calories per serving; in 10 servings, about 491 calories per serving.

VENISON STEW À LA MARCEL

2 pounds of venison stew meat, cut into pieces
2½ tbsp. of olive oil
2 tbsp. of flour
2 large onions, chopped
3 cloves of garlic, minced
2 stalks of celery, chopped
1 medium bell pepper, chopped
2 cups of burgundy wine
¼ cup of fresh lemon juice
½ tsp. of Tabasco sauce
1 tsp. of salt
½ tsp. of freshly ground black pepper
¼ tsp. of white pepper
¼ tsp. of garlic powder

¼ tsp. of onion powder
¼ tsp. of sweet basil
¼ tsp. of thyme
2 bay leaves
½ tsp. of filé powder
6 carrots, cleaned and cut into 1½-inch pieces
12 large mushrooms, sliced
16 small new potatoes with skin, cleaned
1½ cups of Beef Stock (see index for recipe) or beef broth
1 tbsp. of Worcestershire sauce
cooked white rice

In a large heavy pot that has a tight-fitting lid, sauté the meat in the olive oil over medium heat until it is well browned. Remove the meat from the pan, add the flour, and make a brown roux by cooking the flour, stirring constantly, over medium-low heat until it turns a rich, red brown. When the roux is the right color, add the onions, garlic, celery, and bell pepper and cook for 5 minutes. Remove from the heat and let cool for 5 minutes, then add the wine, lemon juice, and Tabasco sauce and mix until blended.

Add the cooked meat along with the salt, black pepper, white pepper, garlic powder, onion powder, sweet basil, thyme, bay leaves, filé powder, carrots, mushrooms, and potatoes. Mix as well as possible, cover the pot, and refrigerate overnight or for 12 hours.

After refrigeration, add the Beef Stock and Worcestershire sauce. Cook over medium heat, stirring often, until the liquid comes to a boil. Reduce the heat to low and simmer, uncovered, for about 1½ hours or until the meat is very tender. Serve hot over cooked white rice. Serves 8.

Lagniappe: As noted in the directions, you can prepare this dish up to the cooking stage and refrigerate it overnight. You can let it sit in the refrigerator for 24 to 36 hours uncooked, but make sure that you stir it every so often.

Another option is to cook the dish completely after following the directions and either refrigerate or freeze it for later use. To reheat, thaw in the refrigerator if frozen, then heat, covered, over low heat until the dish is warmed through, about 15 to 20 minutes. Serve at once. About 271 calories per serving without rice and about 383 calories per serving with ½ cup of cooked white rice.

RABBIT ÉTOUFFÉE

1½ tsp. of salt
¼ tsp. of black pepper
¼ tsp. of red pepper
¼ tsp. of white pepper
½ tsp. of onion powder
¼ tsp. of garlic powder
½ cup of flour
1 rabbit (2½ to 3 pounds),
   cut up into serving pieces
3 tbsp. of shortening

3 large onions, cut into
   slices
¼ cup of finely chopped
   celery
1 tbsp. of minced bell
   pepper
1 clove of garlic, finely
   minced
1 cup of sour cream
¼ tsp. of Tabasco sauce
cooked white rice (optional)

Preheat the oven to 350 degrees. Mix the salt, black pepper, red pepper, white pepper, onion powder, garlic powder, and flour in a mixing bowl. Coat the rabbit pieces well with the flour mixture and set aside.

In a large skillet, melt the shortening over medium heat. Sauté the onions, celery, bell pepper, and garlic until the onions are limp, about 3 minutes. Remove the vegetables from the skillet, being careful to let the shortening drain back into the skillet. Fry the rabbit pieces in the remaining shortening until all sides are golden brown.

Remove from the heat and place the rabbit pieces in a shallow 3- to 3½-quart covered baking dish. Cover the rabbit with the sautéed vegetables and then with the sour cream and Tabasco sauce. Cover and bake for 45 minutes. Uncover the dish and cook for 15 more minutes. Serve hot over cooked white rice if you like, or just the rabbit with the sauce. Serves 4 to 6.

Lagniappe: This is a very versatile dish, for you can substitute chicken, duck, or pork for the rabbit and make other interesting dishes. You can make this dish all the way through the 45-minute covered baking, then refrigerate for later use. If you do, cook the uncovered dish for 20 minutes instead of 15 before serving.

In 4 servings, there are about 750 calories per serving without rice and about 865 calories per serving with ½ cup of cooked white rice. In 6 servings, count on about 499 calories per serving without rice or about 611 calories per serving with rice.

RABBIT CHABLIS

1 tbsp. of butter
1 tbsp. of olive oil
1 clove of garlic, minced
1 medium bay leaf
1 rabbit (2½ pounds), cut into serving pieces
½ cup of chopped onion
1 tbsp. of minced celery
1 tbsp. of minced bell pepper
2 tbsp. of flour

1 cup of Chicken Stock (see index for recipe) or chicken broth
1 cup of Chablis wine
¼ tsp. of Tabasco sauce
¼ tsp. of black pepper
1 tsp. of Worcestershire sauce
salt to taste
cooked white rice

In a large skillet, heat the butter and olive oil until hot. Add the garlic and bay leaf. Sauté the rabbit pieces over medium heat (the skillet should hold the entire rabbit) until the pieces are well browned and the meat is cooked, about 20 minutes. Do not let the meat stick.

Remove the meat, add the onion, celery, and bell pepper, and sauté until the onions are limp and clear, about 3 minutes. Add the flour and stir constantly until it is brown. Do not let it burn. Add the Chicken Stock, Chablis, Tabasco sauce, black pepper, Worcestershire sauce, and salt and blend until the sauce is smooth. Add the rabbit pieces and let the dish simmer for about 15 minutes over low heat. Serve hot over cooked white rice. Serves 4 to 6.

Lagniappe: This dish may be made in advance and refrigerated until you are ready to serve it. Actually, making it in advance improves the dish; this is true for most dishes made from a roux. In 4 servings there are about 505 calories per serving without rice and about 617 calories with ½ cup of cooked white rice. In 6 servings there are about 337 calories per serving without rice or about 449 calories per serving with rice.

Vegetables

This is one of my favorite sections. You can't say too much about vegetables; they either make your main dish a hit or a failure. Vegetables help add variety, contrast, color, and life to any meal. When I was growing up, I can't remember any meal, except sandwiches, that had fewer than three vegetables. I can also easily remember many special meals in which we had as many as seven vegetables.

Good food must not only taste good, it must also look good! Vegetables should be chosen to complement the main dish. Choose vegetables that will contrast with the main dish in color, texture, and flavor. Vegetables should add to the overall ambience of the meal.

Cajuns always ate a lot of vegetables because they were readily available and "dirt cheap." You grew them yourself. The flavors were never in question, because you got them out of your back yard. And because of this abundance, many Cajun dishes called for a lengthy cooking time. This may be contrary to your present way of cooking, but remember, they had such a large amount of free vegetables that they could cook the vegetables down to their very nectar. This lengthy process more often than not changes the original color and texture of the raw vegetable. Yet, since all of the juices remained in the pot and therefore in the dish, great flavorings emerged that created the subtle and exciting tastes that became a Cajun trademark. The recipes in this section that use this style of cooking are: Smothered Cabbage Picard, Baked Collards Marie, Macque Choux, Eggplant Deborah, Stuffed Mirliton Acadie, Mustard Greens and Salt Pork, Creamed Spinach Toussaint, Baked Acorn Squash Bunkie, Squash Nicholas, Squash Hebert, and Stuffed Tomatoes.

Cajuns also dealt with vegetables another way. There is something special about a freshly picked vegetable. I have also included vegetable recipes that allow the vegetable to remain in a form that you can identify. The cooking approach is different, yet the product is equally exciting. Examples of this method are: Fresh Asparagus Spears Dupuis, Fresh Green Beans Eloise, Brussels Sprouts Phillippe, Glazed Carrots Perrine, Cauliflower au Gratin, Braised Celery Pierre, Boiled Whole Okra, Deep Fried Parsley, Fresh Peas and Onions Poirier, Field Peas Gaspar, Parsley-Garlic Fresh New Potatoes, Baked Fresh Sweet Potatoes, and Scalloped Potatoes LaFrance.

The great variety of produce available to us on a daily basis demands creativity. That is what Cajun cooks have always had: the ability to experiment with what was available. Louisiana has always been blessed with a long growing season. In fact, most years it never stops. We aren't even limited by what we can get from our own ground. Today numerous items that were once foreign to our area can be obtained in fresh and quality pickings. Experiment! Don't ever let your cooking become predictable—except predictably great. A cook who works wonders with vegetables will be a cook who succeeds.

Grandma always tried to have at least one favorite vegetable for everyone in a meal (with me she had no trouble), and she always wanted to have a new and exciting one that you just had to try. If the new recipe worked, it was added to the list of favorites. If not, she reworked it and reworked it, but she never gave it up. Somehow, she'd find that little something that would raise it from the mundane to the scrumptious. A pinch of spice here or there would add that pizzazz that was not expected but oh, so good. She liked to surprise us with a medley of flavors, each one exciting and unique.

It is that Cajun excitement that comes from my soul that I have attempted to achieve and share with you in this section. Please note that many recipes give you alternate suggestions and uses. Go with your favorites, but add a little fun to your life and try that something new. Who knows? It may just turn out to be your new family favorite.

ARTICHOKES WILLIE

3 14-ounce cans of artichoke hearts, drained
1 cup of unsalted butter, melted
2 4-ounce cans of sliced mushrooms, drained
½ cup of fresh lemon juice

1 2-ounce jar of pimentos, diced
½ tsp. of Italian seasoning
½ tsp. of salt
¼ tsp. of Tabasco sauce
¼ tsp. of black pepper
½ cup of slivered almonds
paprika

Preheat the oven to 350 degrees. Combine all ingredients except the almonds and paprika in a lightly greased casserole and smooth out the top of the dish. Top with the slivered almonds and sprinkle with the paprika. Bake at 350 degrees for 15 to 20 minutes or until the dish is hot throughout. Serve at once. Serves 8.

Lagniappe: Do not freeze this dish. You can mix all the ingredients together and add the almonds and paprika, then cover tightly with plastic wrap. You can then refrigerate it for as much as 24 hours before baking. About 377 calories per serving. Take it or leave it, but don't change it!

This recipe is from my mother-in-law, Rose LeBlanc.

FRESH ASPARAGUS SPEARS DUPUIS

1 pound of tender fresh asparagus, cleaned and trimmed
water to steam asparagus
3 tbsp. of unsalted butter
1 clove of garlic, minced
¼ cup of minced green onion bottoms
½ tsp. of salt

¼ tsp. of black pepper
¼ tsp. of Tabasco sauce
¼ tsp. of white pepper
1 cup of heavy cream
2 large egg yolks, well beaten
½ tsp. of fresh lemon juice
2 tbsp. of chopped fresh chives

Place the asparagus in a steamer and put enough water in the bottom to bring a nice steam up. Put the steamer over high heat and bring the water to a boil. Once heavy steam appears, steam the asparagus for 30 seconds, then turn the heat off. Leave the steamer on the burner.

In a large skillet, melt the butter over low heat. Add the garlic and green onion bottoms and sauté for 4 minutes. Remove the asparagus from the steamer and drain it on paper towels. Place the asparagus in the skillet and sauté over low heat for 5 minutes. Add the salt, black pepper, Tabasco sauce, and white pepper and blend well. Mix the heavy cream and egg yolks in a mixing bowl. Pour this mixture into the skillet.

Continue to simmer for about 10 more minutes. The sauce should thicken somewhat and the asparagus should be quite tender. Add the lemon juice and chives. Toss well and serve at once. Serves 6.

Lagniappe: A very colorful side dish. The white and green make nice contrasts with many dishes. You may make this dish well in advance, except for the last 5 minutes of simmering the sauce. Cook it for about 5 minutes with the cream and egg yolks, then cover and refrigerate. (Do not freeze this dish.) When you are ready to serve, just simmer it for 5 more minutes, toss it with the lemon juice and chives, and serve hot. Of course, as with any fresh vegetable, it is best eaten right after cooking, but you will be pleased with the quality and texture if you have to let it sit for a few hours in the refrigerator.

   About 227 calories per serving. To reduce the calories to about 141 per serving, simply substitute half-and-half for the heavy cream and follow the directions as above. The sauce will be thinner, but it will still be quite flavorful and the texture will be acceptable.

FRESH GREEN BEANS ELOISE

1 pound of fresh whole
   green beans, cleaned
cold water to cover beans
½ cup of chopped onion
1 tbsp. of diced celery

¼ tsp. of minced garlic
½ pound of salt pork
salt and pepper to taste
1 tbsp. of unsalted butter

   Place the green beans in a large saucepan and cover them with cold water. Add the onion, celery, garlic, and salt pork. Bring to a boil over high heat, then reduce the heat to low and simmer, uncovered, until the beans are tender, about 15 minutes. When the beans are cooked, add the salt and pepper. Toss the beans gently in the butter. Serve at once. Serves 4.

Lagniappe: This was one of my grandmother's best dishes. It is simple, but it is so good. You get all the flavor and freshness of fresh green beans. You can cook it in advance and refrigerate or even freeze it, but to enjoy it to its fullest, eat it right after cooking. To reheat, let it thaw in the refrigerator if frozen, add a little water, and steam it back to life. Serve at once.

About 180 calories per serving if you don't eat the salt pork. The pork has over 1,700 calories per ½ pound. There are two ways to significantly reduce the calories in this dish. You can cut the pork back to 2 ounces and cook as above. This will reduce the calories to about 103 per serving. Or you can leave the salt pork out altogether, substitute 1 tablespoon of bacon drippings for the butter, and cook as above. This will give you about 71 calories per serving.

Both of these alternate methods give excellent results, especially the second one. The bacon drippings tend to blend well with the beans and give you an excellent dish with very few calories.

BRUSSELS SPROUTS PHILLIPPE

1½ pounds of fresh tender young Brussels sprouts
4 tbsp. of unsalted butter
1 tsp. of salt
½ tsp. of Tabasco sauce
¼ tsp. of white pepper
¼ tsp. of black pepper
¼ cup of white wine

¼ cup of fresh lemon juice
1 tbsp. of finely minced celery
1 tbsp. of finely minced carrots
1 tbsp. of finely minced onion
1 clove of garlic, minced

Preheat the oven to 350 degrees. Trim and clean the Brussels sprouts. Melt the butter in a heavy skillet. Sauté the Brussels sprouts in the skillet over medium heat for 7 minutes. Pour the Brussels sprouts and butter into a large casserole that has a tight-fitting cover and add the remaining ingredients. Stir the mixture through to blend all the ingredients together.

Bake at 350 degrees for 40 minutes or until the sprouts are tender. Every 10 minutes or so, remove the cover and stir the dish carefully to prevent any sticking. When the 40 minutes is up, remove the cover, and turn the heat up to 450 degrees, and bake for 5 more minutes. Serve at once. Serves 4 to 6.

Lagniappe: Fresh vegetables should be eaten at once, but if you must, you can freeze or refrigerate this dish. Just thaw in the refrigerator if frozen and bake in a covered casserole dish at 300 degrees for 10 minutes until the dish is heated through. You will lose some of the peak flavor and texture, but the product will still be quite good. About 162 calories per serving in each of 6 servings or 213 calories per serving in each of 4 servings. I don't recommend changing this recipe to reduce the calories.

SMOTHERED CABBAGE PICARD

2½ tbsp. of bacon fat
1 medium onion, chopped
1 head of cabbage, shredded
1½ cups of water
1 tsp. of salt

¼ tsp. of Tabasco sauce
¼ tsp. of black papper
1 tbsp. of sugar
1 strip of bacon, chopped

Melt the bacon fat over medium heat in a large, heavy skillet that has a cover. Add the onion and sauté until limp, about 3 minutes. Add the cabbage and sauté for 5 minutes over medium heat. Add the remaining ingredients, mix well, and cover. Reduce the heat to low and simmer until the cabbage is done, about 45 minutes. Serve hot. Serves 8 to 10.

Lagniappe: Although this dish is best served right after cooking, you can make it in advance and either refrigerate or freeze it. To reheat, thaw in the refrigerator if frozen and cook in a covered skillet until the cabbage is hot. For variety, you can add ham hocks to the cabbage instead of the chopped bacon. Make sure your skillet is large enough to hold the ham hocks and cabbage. About 83 calories per serving in 10 servings and 104 calories per serving in 8 servings. No change recommended.

GLAZED CARROTS PERRINE

1 bunch of fresh, tender
young carrots, cleaned
water to boil carrots
½ tsp. of salt
3 tbsp. of unsalted butter
2 tbsp. of light brown sugar

2 tbsp. of dark brown sugar
¼ tsp. of ginger
¼ tsp. of nutmeg
1 tsp. of fresh lemon juice
½ tsp. of salt

Scrape the outside layer off the carrots gently and cut the carrots diagonally into 1-inch pieces. In a large saucepan, bring the water to boiling and add the ½ teaspoon of salt. Add the carrots and boil over high heat for 5 to 7 minutes until the carrots are tender. Remove from the heat and drain well.

In a heavy skillet over medium heat, melt the butter. Add the carrots and sauté them for 2 minutes, making sure all are coated with the butter. Add the sugars, ginger, and nutmeg. Stir constantly until the sugar is melted and the carrots are coated with the glaze, about 4 minutes. Add the lemon juice and salt and blend well. Serve at once. Serves 4 to 6.

Lagniappe: This recipe should be served right after cooking. If you want to save a little time, you can boil the carrots in advance and refrigerate them for glazing later in the day. You can freeze the dish after it is completely done, but you will lose the peak flavor and texture. If you freeze, thaw in the refrigerator and heat in the microwave on high power just until the carrots are hot, about 2 minutes. Or you can put them back into the skillet and heat over medium heat until the carrots are heated through, about 3 minutes.

About 113 calories for 6 servings or 170 calories for 4 servings. You can reduce the calories by cutting the butter down from 3 tablespoons to 1 tablespoon, adding 1 tablespoon of water, and cutting out the 2 tablespoons of light brown sugar. This will reduce the calories to around 61 per serving in 6 servings or 92 per serving in 4 servings. The glaze will still be excellent, but not as rich.

CAULIFLOWER AU GRATIN

1 large head of cauliflower
water to steam cauliflower
¼ cup of butter
3 tbsp. of flour
1 13-ounce can of
  evaporated milk
¼ cup of milk
4 ounces of American
  cheese, chopped

¼ tsp. of Tabasco sauce
½ tsp. of onion powder
¼ tsp. of black pepper
½ tsp. of salt
2 egg yolks, beaten
butter to grease baking dish
paprika

Clean and wash the cauliflower. Cut off the green leaves and remove the center core. If a steamer is available, place the cauliflower in it with enough water to bring a good steam up. Steam the head for 5 minutes over high heat (or boil it for 4 minutes), then turn the heat off.

Preheat the oven to 350 degrees. In a large saucepan over medium heat, melt the butter. Add the flour, blend well, and cook for 2 minutes, stirring constantly. Remove the pan from the heat and add the evaporated milk and the milk. Blend in, then return to the heat. As the sauce thickens and gets smooth, add the cheese, Tabasco sauce, onion powder, black pepper, and salt. Reduce the heat to low and cook until all the cheese has melted.

Spoon some of the hot mixture into the bowl containing the beaten eggs. Continue doing this until the egg mixture is warm and smooth. Pour it into the saucepan, blend, and remove the sauce from the heat. Arrange the cauliflower flowerets nicely in a greased baking dish. Pour the sauce over the flowerets and sprinkle with paprika. Bake at 350 degrees for 30 minutes; the sauce should be bubbling. Serve hot. Serves 8 to 10.

Lagniappe: This dish may be made in advance and put in the refrigerator or freezer. You can completely cook the dish and freeze it or make the dish up to the baking part and refrigerate it until you are ready to serve. If you freeze it, thaw the dish in the refrigerator and heat it in the microwave at high power for 45 seconds until hot, or bake it at 350 degrees until the sauce begins to bubble again, about 10 to 12 minutes.

This is an excellent recipe to use for other au gratin dishes. You can substitute broccoli, onions, cabbage, or asparagus and just make the recipe as above. About 168 calories per serving in 10 servings or about 211 calories per serving in 8 servings. This makes a rich cheese sauce that is so good that I don't suggest any changes.

BRAISED CELERY PIERRE

1 bunch of celery (about 1½ pounds)
2½ tbsp. of peanut oil
3 cloves of garlic, minced
3 tbsp. of minced carrot
2 tbsp. of minced onion
½ cup of dry white wine

½ cup of Chicken Stock (see index for recipe) or chicken broth
½ tsp. of Tabasco sauce
½ tsp. of salt
¼ tsp. of white pepper
2 tbsp. of finely minced fresh parsley

Trim the celery, cutting off all bad pieces and pulling off the hard strings. Cut the celery into 4-inch lengths. Heat the peanut oil in a heavy iron skillet over medium heat until it is hot. Add the celery pieces and sauté them until they brown slightly, about 7 minutes. Add the garlic, carrot, and onion and sauté for 3 minutes over medium heat. Add the wine, Chicken Stock, Tabasco sauce, salt, and white pepper and bring to a boil. Be sure to scrape the bottom of the pot carefully to get any browned pieces dissolved into the liquid.

Let the mixture boil for 3 minutes, then reduce the heat to low and let it simmer slowly until the majority of the liquid is reduced, about 30 minutes. Arrange the celery nicely on a serving plate and pour the remaining sauce over it. Sprinkle with the parsley and serve at once. Serves 6.

Lagniappe: Like any other fresh vegetable dish, this should be served right after it is cooked. You can freeze this dish; although you will lose a bit of flavor and texture, it will still be quite nice.

Another shortcut would be to make the dish completely through the simmering, but stop the simmering process after 20 minutes. Let the dish cool, then cover it and refrigerate. When you are ready to serve, bring the liquid to a hard boil over medium heat. Reduce the heat and let it simmer for 10 more minutes, then serve at once.

If you freeze the dish, you can put it right into the microwave frozen and heat on high power for 4 minutes. Be sure the container is covered with plastic wrap and has a small hole for the steam to get out. You can also cover the dish with aluminum foil and heat it in the oven for 20 minutes at 350 degrees. Only about 88 calories per serving.

BAKED COLLARDS MARIE

2 pounds of fresh collard greens
butter to grease casserole dish
2 tbsp. of olive oil
1 tsp. of salt

½ tsp. of Tabasco sauce
¼ tsp. of black pepper
1 tsp. of minced garlic
½ cup of bread crumbs
2 pats of butter, cut into pieces

Preheat the oven to 375 degrees. Wash the collard greens well, chop them into fine pieces, and put them in a large mixing bowl. Grease a large casserole dish with butter. Put the olive oil, salt, Tabasco sauce, black pepper, and garlic into the bowl with the greens and mix thoroughly. Pour this mixture into the casserole dish and pack it down well. Sprinkle the bread crumbs over the top of the casserole and dot it with the butter. Bake at 375 degrees for 1 hour. The top should be crusty and light brown and the greens tender. Serve hot. Serves 6 to 8.

Lagniappe: Although this fresh vegetable dish should be served right after it is cooked for maximum flavor and texture, I find that it does freeze quite well. You may also refrigerate before use.

From the refrigerator, cover the dish lightly with foil and heat it at 300 degrees for about 15 minutes. From the freezer, put it frozen into the microwave, lightly covered, and heat it on high power for 4 to 5 minutes. You can also thaw it in the refrigerator and cook as from the refrigerator or cover it tightly with foil and heat it in the oven right from the freezer at 350 degrees for 25 minutes. Serve this dish hot. About 120 calories in each of 8 servings or about 160 calories in each of 6 servings.

MACQUE CHOUX
(SMOTHERED CORN)

12 fresh, sweet ears of corn	1 tbsp. of sugar
1 large onion, chopped	¼ tsp. of Tabasco sauce
1 medium bell pepper, chopped	salt to taste
	¼ tsp. of black pepper
2 large tomatoes, skinned and chopped	2 tbsp. of cooking oil
	1 tbsp. of unsalted butter
1 clove of garlic, minced	

Cut the corn off each cob by standing the ear on end and scraping the kernels off from the middle to the bottom of the ear with a downward motion all around, then repeating for the other end of the ear. Make sure you scrape all of the milk from the cob. Repeat for all 12 ears.

Mix the corn, onion, bell pepper, tomatoes, and garlic together. Add the sugar, Tabasco sauce, salt, and black pepper. In a large skillet that has a lid, heat the oil over medium heat. Melt the butter, then add the vegetable mixture. Cook for 5 minutes, stirring constantly to keep the dish from sticking. Reduce heat to low and let the dish simmer, covered, for about 20 minutes or until the corn is tender. Serve hot. Serves 6 to 8.

Lagniappe: This dish (pronounced "mock shoe") may be made in advance if you like and refrigerated until you are ready to use. It also freezes well. Reheat it after thawing in a covered skillet over low heat. This was one of my grandmother's specialties; it has always been one of my favorites. I like it cold or hot. About 181 calories in each of 8 servings, or about 283 in each of 6 servings.

EGGPLANT DEBORAH

2 large eggplants, 1 peeled,
both cut into fourths
water to cover eggplant
1 tsp. of salt
4 strips of bacon, chopped
1 stick of unsalted butter
1 large onion, chopped
1 medium bell pepper,
chopped
1 stalk of celery, diced
1 clove of garlic, minced

½ tsp. of Tabasco sauce
¼ tsp. of garlic powder
½ tsp. of onion powder
⅛ tsp. of sweet basil
1 tsp. of lemon juice
2½ cups of Ritz cracker
crumbs
salt and pepper to taste
¼ cup of plain bread crumbs
2 pats of butter, cut into
pieces

Preheat the oven to 350 degrees. Place the eggplant in a large saucepan and cover with water. Add the teaspoon of salt and bring the water to a boil over high heat. Boil for 1 minute, then turn off the heat. Let the eggplant sit in the water until you are ready to use it.

In another large saucepan or skillet, sauté the bacon until it is brown and crisp, but do not burn it. Melt the butter in the saucepan with the bacon, then add the onion, bell pepper, celery, and garlic. Sauté for 4 minutes over medium heat or until the onions are clear. Remove the eggplant from the water with a slotted spoon (do not worry about draining all the water) and place it in the skillet. Sauté for 5 minutes. Season with Tabasco sauce, garlic powder, onion powder, sweet basil, and lemon juice.

Blend in the cracker crumbs and salt and pepper to taste. Pour into a casserole dish. Sprinkle lightly with the bread crumbs and dot with butter. Bake at 350 degrees for 30 minutes. Serve hot. Serves 8.

Lagniappe: This is an exceptional dish. You can make it completely in advance and either freeze or refrigerate it for later use. To cook, just thaw in the refrigerator if frozen and bake at 350 degrees for 12 to 15 minutes.

It is also a wonderful base. Add ham, chicken, shrimp, oysters, or crabmeat to it for a very special main dish. You can even freeze the dish after you add the seafood or meat and it keeps very well. I usually freeze it in a casserole dish that can go right into the oven for a quick and easy taste treat. As listed above, the recipe has about 350 calories per serving, but don't you change it one bit; it's too good as it is!

STUFFED MIRLITON ACADIE

6 mirlitons (vegetable pears)
water to steam mirlitons
2 strips of bacon, chopped
5 tbsp. of unsalted butter
1 stalk of celery, minced
1 onion, finely chopped
1 small sweet red bell
  pepper, minced
3 cloves of garlic, minced
1½ cups of diced baked ham
1 pound of shrimp, coarsely
  chopped

½ cup of Ritz cracker
  crumbs
½ tsp. of Tabasco sauce
1 tsp. of Worcestershire
  sauce
1 tsp. of Seafood Seasoning
  Mix (see index for recipe)
1 tsp. of fresh lemon juice
½ cup of seasoned bread
  crumbs
2 pats of butter, cut into
  pieces

Steam the mirlitons by bringing the water in a steamer to a boil. Once the water has begun to boil, steam for 3 minutes, then turn off the heat. Let the mirlitons stay in the steamer until you are ready for them. In a large, heavy saucepan over medium heat, fry the bacon until it is brown and crisp. Remove from the heat, add the unsalted butter, and set aside. Cut each mirliton in half and remove the seed. Scoop out the center of the mirliton with a spoon or a melon baller, taking care not to tear through the outer shell. The scooped-out pieces should be the size of a ½-inch melon baller. Return the bacon-butter sauce to the stove over medium heat. When hot, add the scooped-out mirliton, celery, onion, red bell pepper, and garlic. Sauté these vegetables for 15 minutes, stirring often to prevent them from sticking.

Preheat the oven to 350 degrees. Add the ham, shrimp, and cracker crumbs to the vegetables and blend well. Add the Tabasco sauce, Worcestershire sauce, Seafood Seasoning Mix and lemon juice and mix in well. Stuff equal amounts of the stuffing mix into the mirliton halves. Sprinkle the bread crumbs over the stuffing and dot each mound of stuffing with butter. Bake at 350 degrees for 30 minutes. Serve hot. Serves 12 as a vegetable or 6 as a main dish.

Lagniappe: This is really a treat! If you have trouble finding mirlitons at your grocery store, ask for vegetable pears (the name they go by away from Louisiana). This dish may be made in advance up to the baking stage; just cover and refrigerate until you are ready to bake (up to 12 hours). You can also completely bake the dish and freeze it, shell and all. To reheat, just thaw and place in the oven, uncovered, at 350 degrees for 12 to 15 minutes. Serve hot.

You can use this as an excellent complement to any meal. The stuffing and the green shell make for an excellent contrast. As a main dish, serve 2 halves per person and just wait for the smiles. If you like, you can substitute smoked sausage for the ham and crabmeat or oysters for the shrimp. This will give you any number of combinations, all equally exciting.

In 12 servings (as a vegetable), the dish has about 237 calories per serving. Each of 6 main-dish servings has about 475 calories. To reduce the calories in the vegetable serving to 188 each and in the main-dish serving to 334, make the following substitutions: use only 2 tablespoons of butter in the stuffing instead of 5, use only ½ cup of ham instead of 1½ cups, use 1½ pounds of shrimp instead of only 1 pound, and do not dot the mirlitons with butter. Cook and bake as directed. Although it will not be as rich and filling a dish, it will still be excellent.

MUSTARD GREENS AND SALT PORK

2 bunches of mustard greens
water to cover greens
1 pound of salt pork, cut into 2-inch pieces
1 tsp. of salt

½ tsp. of Tabasco sauce
1 tsp. of sugar
¼ cup of minced onion
¼ tsp. of black pepper

Soak the greens in water for 20 minutes, then clean each green, cutting off any thick stems or bad pieces. Place the greens in a large, heavy pot and add enough water to cover. Add the pork, salt, Tabasco sauce, sugar, onion, and black pepper and bring the mixture to a boil over high heat. Let it boil for 2 minutes, then reduce the heat to low and simmer the mixture, covered, for 20 to 30 minutes until the greens are tender.

Remove the greens and bring the pot liquor to a hard boil. Boil until the liquid is reduced by ⅔, then return the greens to the pot for 1 minute to reheat them. Pour into a serving dish and serve at once. Serves 6 to 8.

Lagniappe: This dish freezes well and actually improves in flavor when you let it stand in the refrigerator for a few hours or more. To reheat, just thaw if frozen and heat in a pot over medium heat until the greens are hot, about 5 to 7 minutes. This dish is great with plenty of fresh, hot corn bread. You can also substitute turnip greens, collard greens, or Swiss chard in the same recipe to make a variety of dishes. (You may have to increase cooking time for the collard greens and the Swiss chard.)

This is a good dish for the calorie-conscious. Six servings divide up to about 75 calories each, and 8 servings divide up to about 63 calories each—that is, if you do not eat the salt pork that is used for flavoring. If you do eat the pork, it will run about 888 calories per ¼ pound. So to make this a really low-calorie delight, just eat the greens.

BOILED WHOLE OKRA

1 pound of fresh small okra
1 quart of water
1½ tsp. of salt
1½ tsp. of baking powder
¼ tsp. of Tabasco sauce
¼ tsp. of black pepper
1 tbsp. of vinegar
1 tbsp. of lightly salted
butter, melted

Clean the okra and cut the stems off, leaving the caps. Place the okra in a saucepan and add the water, salt, and baking powder. Boil the okra over medium-high heat for 20 minutes or until tender. While the okra is boiling, mix in a small bowl the Tabasco sauce, black pepper, vinegar, and butter. When the okra is cooked, strain the water completely from the saucepan and add the seasoned butter mixture. Toss to coat the okra. Serve at once. Serves 4.

Lagniappe: This dish can be made in advance, refrigerated, and reheated, tightly covered, in the oven or in the microwave. The baking powder is added to keep the nice green color. Okra also freezes well, so you can freeze the completed dish for later use. Let it defrost in the refrigerator, then reheat it in the microwave or in the oven. Of course, as with every fresh vegetable, it should be eaten when at its freshest, right after it is cooked. About 66 calories per serving.

CAJUN FRIED ONION RINGS

2 large onions, peeled
1 cup of milk
¼ tsp. of Tabasco sauce
¼ tsp. of Worcestershire
  sauce
½ cup of flour

1½ tsp. of Chicken
  Seasoning Mix (see
  index for recipe)
cooking oil for deep-frying
salt to taste

Slice the onions about ⅜ inch thick; separate the circles into rings and place them in a large bowl. Mix the milk, Tabasco sauce, and Worcestershire sauce and pour over the onion rings. Soak the rings for 45 minutes to 1 hour.

When the soaking time is up, put the flour and Chicken Seasoning Mix into a medium-sized paper bag and shake well until the seasoning is mixed in with the flour. Add a handful of onion rings at a time to the bag and shake until the rings are well coated with flour. Deep-fry the rings in medium-hot cooking oil that is deep enough to hold all of them. Drain on paper towels and salt to taste. Serve at once. Serves 4 to 6.

Lagniappe: About all you can do in advance to this recipe is prepare the onion rings and let them soak in the milk mixture. You can soak them for longer than 1 hour if you need to. Serve the onion rings right after they are cooked. They do not hold up long and do not reheat well. About 450 calories per serving in 6 servings and about 650 calories per serving with 4 servings. If you want fried onion rings, throw the calorie book away and diet tomorrow!

STUFFED YELLOW ONIONS ROBICHAUD

4 large yellow onions, unpeeled
water to cover onions
2 tsp. of salt
½ pound of fresh pork sausage
¼ cup of chopped bell pepper
¼ cup of finely minced carrot
2 cloves of garlic, minced
2 tbsp. of minced celery
6 large mushrooms, finely chopped

1 cup of French bread, diced small
½ cup of chopped green onion tops
½ tsp. of Tabasco sauce
1 tbsp. of finely minced fresh parsley
3 tbsp. of bread crumbs
1 cup of Beef Stock (see index for recipe) or beef broth
½ cup of dry white wine

Place the onions in a saucepan large enough for all 4 of them to fit on the bottom. Cover with water and add 1 teaspoon of salt. Bring to a boil over high heat and boil for 3 minutes. When the 3 minutes have passed, remove the saucepan from the heat and let the onions cool.

In another saucepan over medium heat, fry the sausage until it has browned well. Remove from the heat and remove all of the fat except about 2 tablespoons. The onions should be somewhat cool by now. Remove them from the water and take off the outer skins. Cut off the bottom of each so the onions will sit flat and you have removed the root from the bottom. Cut off the tops just enough to make the onions uniform. Scoop out the center of the onion with a melon baller or a spoon, leaving about ⅜ inch of the shell all around the center.

Chop the onion that has been removed and add it to the sausage. Add the bell pepper, carrot, garlic, celery, and mushrooms. Return the sausage pot to the stove over medium heat and sauté the vegetables for 5 minutes, stirring often to keep the mixture from sticking. Preheat the oven to 425 degrees. Add the French bread, green onion tops, the other teaspoon of salt, and Tabasco sauce and blend in well. Mix the parsley and bread crumbs and set aside.

Place equal portions of the stuffing mixture into the center of the onions, pressing the mixture down so that it is firmly packed. Place the onions in a shallow baking dish and pour the Beef Stock and wine around them. Place 1 tablespoon of the bread crumb mixture on top of each onion and lightly press it into the stuffing. Cover the pan loosely with foil and bake at 425 degrees for 30 minutes. Remove the foil, reduce the heat to 350 degrees, and bake for 40 minutes.

During the 40 minutes, baste the onions with the liquid every 10 minutes. Serve hot with a little of the liquid from the pan spooned over each onion. Serves 4.

Lagniappe: This dish may be made in advance and either refrigerated or frozen for later use. Thaw in the refrigerator if frozen and bake at 350 degrees, loosely covered, for 15 minutes. About 460 calories per serving as is. Substituting ground round for the pork sausage will reduce the dish to about 280 calories.

DEEP-FRIED PARSLEY

1 bunch of fresh parsley   ¼ tsp. of red pepper
cooking oil for deep-frying   ¼ tsp. of white pepper
1 tsp. of salt

Wash the parsley well and cut off the thick stems from the ends. Heat the oil to about 400 degrees. Arrange the parsley loosely in a deep-frying basket. Drop the parsley into the hot oil and cook for about 1 to 1½ minutes. Pick up the basket, let it drain over the oil for a minute, then dump the parsley out on paper towels to drain. Mix the salt, red pepper, and white pepper. Sprinkle the hot parsley with this seasoning mix and serve at once. Serves 4 to 8.

Lagniappe: No reason to do this recipe in advance, since it only takes a few minutes. Do not try to reheat the parsley; it must be served immediately after it is fried. It is light and melts in your mouth. The flavor is exceptional. It also makes an excellent garnish to add color to a plate.

When well drained, 8 servings have about 130 calories each, 6 servings have about 184 calories each, and 4 servings have about 276 calories each. There really isn't much that you can do to reduce the calories, since this is just parsley and oil. You can be sure of getting as much oil off the parsley as possible by heating the oil as above and draining the parsley well on paper towels.

FRESH PEAS AND ONIONS POIRIER

1 cup of small boiling
  onions, unpeeled
water to cover onions
2½ cups of shelled fresh
  early peas
water to cover onions and
  peas
½ tsp. of salt
2 tbsp. of unsalted butter

1¼ tbsp. of flour
½ tsp. of salt
¼ tsp. of Tabasco sauce
¼ tsp. of white pepper
1 cup of evaporated milk
2 tbsp. of Chicken Stock (see
  index for recipe) or
  chicken broth

Place the onions in a medium saucepan and cover with water. Bring the water to a hard boil over high heat. Reduce heat to a rolling boil and boil the onions for 15 minutes. When finished boiling, remove the onions and peel off the brown outer skin. Empty the onion water and clean out the saucepan. Place the onions and peas in the saucepan. Cover with water and add ½ teaspoon of salt. Bring water to a boil over high heat, then reduce the heat to medium and boil for 12 minutes.

In another saucepan, melt the butter over low heat. Add the flour, blend it in well, and cook, stirring constantly, for 2 minutes. Add the other ½ teaspoon of salt, Tabasco sauce, white pepper, evaporated milk, and Chicken Stock. Blend until the sauce is smooth and creamy, then set aside. When the peas and onions are finished boiling, drain them well. Mix the peas and onions with the cream sauce and bring the dish to a simmer, but do not let it boil. Pour into a serving dish and serve at once. Serves 4 to 6.

Lagniappe: This dish may be made in advance and placed in the refrigerator. To reheat, place in a saucepan over low heat and heat until the peas and onions are warmed, about 5 minutes. You can also freeze it, but some of the quality and texture will be lost. Just thaw in the refrigerator and follow the previous directions for reheating. About 160 calories in each of 6 servings or about 260 calories in each of 4 servings. No reduction in calories is recommended.

FIELD PEAS GASPAR

2 strips of bacon, chopped
1 onion, chopped
¼ cup of chopped bell
  pepper
1 tbsp. of celery, minced
1 clove of garlic, minced

1 tomato, skinned and
  chopped
1 16-ounce can of field peas
¼ tsp. of Tabasco sauce
½ tsp. of salt
⅛ tsp. of black pepper
¼ tsp. of onion powder

Sauté the bacon in a medium saucepan over medium heat until it is crisp and brown. Add the onion, bell pepper, celery, and garlic. Sauté until the onions are clear and limp, about 4 minutes. Add the tomato and sauté for 2 minutes.

Raise the heat to high and pour all the liquid from the can of field peas into the saucepan, taking care not to let the peas drop in. Cook over high heat for 2 minutes. The liquid should reduce by almost half. Add the field peas, Tabasco sauce, salt, black pepper, and onion powder. Reduce the heat to low and simmer for about 3 minutes. Serve hot. Serves 4.

Lagniappe: This is a quick side dish that is easy to cook and serve. If you have any leftovers, they may be refrigerated or frozen for later use. Heat the thawed peas in a covered pan over low heat. This recipe adds much to canned peas and makes them much more appealing. About 185 calories per serving. To reduce the calories to about 130 per serving, simply use half a strip of bacon instead of 2 strips and cook as above.

PARSLEY-GARLIC FRESH NEW POTATOES

16 small fresh new potatoes	½ tsp. of sweet basil
1 tbsp. of olive oil	1 bay leaf, crushed
4 cloves of garlic, minced	1 tbsp. of unsalted butter
½ tsp. of salt	½ cup of minced fresh
½ tsp. of freshly ground	parsley
black pepper	½ tsp. of Tabasco sauce
¼ tsp. of white pepper	

Wash the potatoes well under cold water. If any spots need to be cut off, cut them as thinly as possible. In a very heavy skillet that has a cover, heat the olive oil over high heat until very hot, but do not let it smoke. Add the potatoes and cook over high heat for 3 minutes, constantly stirring to be sure the potatoes don't stick. This will lightly brown the potatoes and help to hold in all their natural juices.

Reduce the heat to medium-low. Add the garlic, salt, black pepper, white pepper, sweet basil, and bay leaf. Sauté, stirring constantly, for 6 minutes. The potatoes will be browned well on all sides. Add the butter, parsley, and Tabasco sauce. Reduce the heat to low, cover the skillet, and simmer for 10 minutes, shaking the skillet every few minutes. Serve at once. Serves 4.

Lagniappe: This dish is best eaten right after it is cooked, but you can make it a few hours ahead. Leave it in the heavy skillet at room temperature. When ready to serve, simply heat the dish over low heat until the potatoes are warmed through, about 4 to 6 minutes. Serve at once.

Do not stir the dish too much, as it will tend to break the potatoes apart. It is best to shake the skillet gently to get the potatoes to move around. Be sure to toss them well—but carefully—just before serving them. This dish makes a nice contrast to many main dishes, with the red potato skin covered with green parsley. About 142 calories per serving.

SCALLOPED POTATOES LAFRANCE

4 large red new potatoes
water to cover potatoes
1 tsp. of salt
¼ tsp. of Tabasco sauce
butter to grease au gratin
   dish
1 clove of garlic, finely
   minced
1 tbsp. of finely minced
   onion

1 cup of milk
½ tsp. of salt
¼ tsp. of white pepper
¼ tsp. of red pepper
¼ cup of heavy cream
3 pats of butter, cut into
   pieces
½ tsp. of finely minced fresh
   parsley
¼ tsp. of paprika

Clean and wash the potatoes and place them in a large saucepan. Cover them with water and add the teaspoon of salt and Tabasco sauce. Bring the water to a boil over high heat, then reduce to low. Simmer for 5 minutes, then remove from the heat and drain.

Preheat the oven to 425 degrees. Butter the bottom of a large au gratin dish, then sprinkle the garlic and onion evenly over the bottom. Slice the potatoes neatly (do not peel) and arrange them in layers. Mix the milk, the ½ tsp. of salt, white pepper and red pepper until well blended, then pour the mixture over the potatoes. Let it soak in for a minute, then pour the heavy cream over them evenly.

Dot with butter and sprinkle with the parsley and paprika. Bake at 425 degrees for 20 minutes, then reduce the heat to 350 degrees and bake for 40 more minutes. Serve hot. Serves 6.

Lagniappe: For best results, this dish can only be served right after it is made. Do not freeze, and do not refrigerate after baking. You will lose both texture and quality. About 162 calories per serving. No changes are recommended.

CAJUN FRENCH FRIES

3 large white potatoes
ice water to cover potatoes
cooking oil for deep-frying
  (peanut oil is best)
1 tsp. of salt

¼ tsp. of black pepper
¼ tsp. of red pepper
¼ tsp. of onion powder
¼ tsp. of dry hot mustard

Peel the potatoes and cut them into long strips about ½ inch thick. Soak them in a large bowl of ice water for 5 minutes to remove the starch from their surfaces. Remove the fries and drain on paper towels.

Heat the oil to about 325 degrees in a deep fryer. Place half of the potatoes in the frying basket and fry them for about 2½ minutes. The potatoes should be somewhat cooked, but not brown. Remove from the oil, let the fries drain over the fryer for a minute, and dump the fries out onto a pile of paper towels. Repeat the process with the remaining fries.

Allow the fries to stand for about 10 minutes after the first cooking. Raise the fryer heat to 400 degrees. When the oil is hot, put half of the fries at a time back into the fryer. You will need to cook them for about 4 more minutes until they are nicely browned, draining them on more paper towels after cooking. Repeat for the remaining fries.

While the fries are cooking, mix the salt, black pepper, red pepper, onion powder and dry hot mustard. When the fries are cooked, sprinkle the seasoning mixture lightly over them, taking care to toss them so they are evenly seasoned. Serve at once. Serves 6.

Lagniappe: French fries are a big part of the Cajun scene. They add much to many fried seafood meals and are a nice complement to many meat dishes as well. You can cut the fries, take them through their first cooking, and set them aside, covered, at room temperature for a few hours before the final cooking. This will save time in preparation when you are trying to coordinate all your dishes for one final serving time. About 375 calories per serving, and there is not a thing you can do to change it!

CREAMED FRESH SPINACH TOUSSAINT

1½ pounds of fresh spinach
water to cover spinach
½ tsp. of salt
½ tsp. of Tabasco sauce
½ stick of unsalted butter
1 8-ounce package of cream
   cheese, softened

1 cup of seasoned bread
   crumbs
½ tsp. of salt
¼ tsp. of black pepper
¼ tsp. of Tabasco sauce
butter to grease baking dish

Preheat the oven to 350 degrees. Wash the spinach and cut off the thick stems. Roll two or three spinach leaves together lightly and cut them into fine shreds (chiffonade). Repeat the process until all the spinach is chopped.

Place the chiffonade of spinach in a large saucepot and cover with water. Add the ½ teaspoon of salt and the ½ teaspoon of Tabasco sauce and bring to a boil over high heat. When the water begins to boil, cook 1 minute, then remove the pot from the heat. Let the spinach stand in the hot water for 1 more minute before you drain it.

In a large, heavy skillet, melt the butter over medium heat. Add the drained cooked spinach and sauté in the butter for 2 minutes. Add the softened cream cheese and continue to heat until the cheese is melted, stirring constantly to keep it from sticking. Add the bread crumbs and blend in well. Add the other ½ teaspoon of salt, the black pepper, and the ¼ teaspoon of Tabasco sauce and mix in. Pour the dish into a lightly greased baking dish and bake at 350 degrees for 15 minutes. Serve hot. Serves 6 to 8.

Lagniappe: This dish should be eaten right after cooking, but it can be made in advance and frozen or refrigerated without a tragic loss of texture or quality. Thaw in the refrigerator if frozen and bake at 300 degrees for 10 minutes until the dish is warm. Serve at once.

About 223 calories in each of 8 servings and about 297 calories in each of 6 servings. You can cut the cream cheese down to 4 ounces and the bread crumbs down to ½ cup, which will reduce the calories to about 150 calories each for 8 servings and about 200 calories each for 6 servings. This alteration will make the dish much less creamy, and the gratin will not be as crusty.

BAKED ACORN SQUASH BUNKIE

2 medium acorn squash
water
3 tbsp. of butter
½ tsp. of nutmeg
¼ tsp. of ginger

¼ tsp. of cinnamon
3 tbsp. of dark brown sugar
2 tbsp. of light brown sugar
4 tsp. of dark brown sugar

Preheat the oven to 350 degrees. Cut the 2 squash in half. Scoop out the seeds and stringy pieces with a spoon. Place the squash halves flat side down in a baking pan and add about 1½ inches of water. bake at 350 degrees for 35 minutes. Remove from the oven and let the squash halves cool for a few moments so you can handle them. Raise the oven temperature to 450 degrees.

Scoop out most of the meat from the squash, taking care not to tear the sides, and put it in a large bowl. Add the butter, nutmeg, ginger, cinnamon, the 3 tablespoons of dark brown sugar, and light brown sugar. Blend very well; the butter should melt and be absorbed. Spoon equal amounts of mixture into the shells. You may have to crumple a bit of foil to form a basket around the squash to keep the shells from turning over in the baking dish, or you can put them in a dish that is just the right size to hold the shells upright.

Sprinkle 1 teaspoon of dark brown sugar over each half and place in the oven at 450 degrees for 10 minutes. Reduce the heat to 350 degrees and bake for 30 minutes. Serve at once. Serves 4.

Lagniappe: You can bake this dish completely in advance, then refrigerate for later use. To reheat, just put in a 350-degree oven for 15 minutes. Or you can follow the recipe up to the refilling of the shells, then refrigerate and bake as directed when you are almost ready to serve. This recipe also freezes well. Simply thaw in the refrigerator and follow the reheating directions above.

About 270 calories per serving. To reduce the calories to around 160 per serving and still have a nice dish, follow the recipe above but omit the butter, the 3 tablespoons of dark brown sugar, and the light brown sugar. Sprinkle each shell with 1 teaspoon of dark brown sugar and bake as above.

SQUASH NICHOLAS

1½ pounds of tender yellow squash, washed
water to steam squash
3 strips of bacon, chopped
½ stick of unsalted butter
⅛ cup of olive oil
1 large onion, chopped
½ cup of chopped bell pepper
¼ cup of diced celery
1 clove of garlic, minced
½ tsp. of Tabasco sauce

1 tsp. of Worcestershire sauce
¼ tsp. of garlic powder
¼ tsp. of onion powder
⅛ cup of minced fresh parsley
1½ cups of Ritz cracker crumbs
salt and pepper to taste
⅛ cup of seasoned bread crumbs
1 pat of butter, cut into pieces

Preheat the oven to 350 degrees. Put the squash into a steamer and bring the water to a boil over high heat. Once the water is boiling, steam for 3 minutes. Remove from the heat, but leave the squash in the steamer.

In a large saucepan, sauté the bacon until it is brown and crisp. Add the ½ stick of butter and olive oil. When the butter melts, add the onion, bell pepper, celery, and garlic. Sauté for 3 to 5 minutes over medium heat until the vegetables are clear and limp.

As the vegetables are sautéing, remove the squash (be careful; they will be quite hot) and cut them into ¼-inch-thick circles. Put the sliced squash back into the saucepan and sauté for 5 more minutes. Add the Tabasco sauce, Worcestershire sauce, garlic powder, onion powder, parsley, and cracker crumbs and blend well. Salt and pepper to taste. Pour into a shallow casserole dish and lightly sprinkle with the bread crumbs. Dot with the pat of butter and bake at 350 degrees for 30 minutes. Serve hot. Serves 6 to 8.

Lagniappe: Although this recipe is at its prime when it is first cooked, it does take well to refrigerating or freezing. Freeze it in an ovenproof dish to save time and effort. Just thaw in the refrigerator if frozen and heat at 350 degrees for 12 to 15 minutes. Serve hot. About 240 calories per serving in 8 servings or about 320 calories per serving in 6 servings. Leave this recipe alone and make it just as it is; you'll be glad you did.

SQUASH HEBERT

1 pound of tender yellow squash, washed	½ tsp. of cinnamon
	½ tsp. of nutmeg
3 tbsp. of unsalted butter	½ tsp. of ginger
½ cup of sugar	1 tbsp. of dark brown sugar

Cut the squash into circles about ½ inch thick. Melt the butter over medium heat in a heavy saucepan. Add the squash and sauté for 5 minutes, stirring constantly. Add the remaining ingredients and sauté until the solids are dissolved, stirring constantly. Reduce the heat to low and simmer for 10 minutes. Serve hot. Serves 4 to 6.

Lagniappe: This is a quick and easy vegetable dish that was one of my grandmother's favorites. This squash lends itself well to sweetness. The rich brown and yellow color of the dish has eye appeal and makes a nice contrast on a plate that needs other colors to make it more appealing.

You can make this dish completely in advance and store it in the refrigerator for later use without hurting the quality of the dish much. It also freezes quite well; just thaw in the refrigerator and heat over low heat until it is hot. About 138 calories per serving in 6 servings and 207 calories per serving in 4 servings. No change is recommended.

BAKED FRESH SWEET POTATOES

6 medium sweet potatoes, washed
water to boil potatoes
1 tsp. of salt
butter to grease casserole dish
½ cup of dark brown sugar
¼ cup of light brown sugar
1 tsp. of cinnamon
½ tsp. of nutmeg
½ tsp. of ginger
¼ tsp. of ground cloves
½ tbsp. of fresh lemon juice
2 tbsp. of unsalted butter, melted
½ cup of pecan pieces
2 cups of miniature marshmallows

Place the sweet potatoes in a large pot and cover 1 inch above with water. Add the salt and bring to a boil over high heat. When the water begins to boil, reduce the heat to medium and boil for 30 minutes. Remove from the heat and drain.

Preheat oven to 300 degrees. When the potatoes are cool enough to handle, peel them and chop them into 1-inch pieces. Place the potato pieces in a greased large casserole dish. Mix the dark brown sugar, light brown sugar, cinnamon, nutmeg, ginger, and cloves and sprinkle the mixture over the potatoes. Pour the fresh lemon juice evenly over all, then do the same with the butter.

Sprinkle the pecan pieces evenly around the dish, then cover with the marshmallows. Bake at 300 degrees for 30 minutes. The tops of the marshmallows should be golden brown. Serve hot. Serves 8.

Lagniappe: This dish may be completely made in advance and frozen or refrigerated. To reheat, just thaw in the refrigerator if frozen and bake at 300 degrees for 12 to 15 minutes until the potatoes are hot. You can also prepare the recipe up to the baking and freeze or refrigerate until you are ready to use. If you follow this method, bake the dish for 30 minutes at 300 degrees. The only drawback to the second method is that it can make the dish more watery sometimes. It seems that the potatoes do retain water at times and, if frozen uncooked, may bleed this water into the dish. Be sure to cover the dish tightly before freezing no matter which method you use.

This recipe has about 363 calories per serving. There really isn't anything that you can do to reduce the calories and still keep the dish intact. Go ahead; enjoy yourself!

STUFFED TOMATOES

5 firm, red tomatoes
20 large mushrooms
1 bunch of green onions, cleaned
1 small bell pepper
2 cloves of garlic
1 stalk of celery
1 small onion
½ cup of chopped fresh parsley
2 strips of bacon, chopped
3 tbsp. of olive oil

3 tbsp. of unsalted butter
¼ cup of Romano cheese
¼ cup of Parmesan cheese
¾ cup of Italian bread crumbs
¼ tsp. of Tabasco sauce
1 tbsp. of Worcestershire sauce
½ tsp. of salt
¼ tsp. of black pepper
1 tsp. of fresh lemon juice

Preheat the oven to 500 degrees. Trim the dark parts off both ends of the tomatoes, then cut the tomatoes in half across. Scoop out the center of each tomato, taking care not to tear the sides, and discard the pulp.

Chop the mushrooms, green onions, bell pepper, garlic, celery, onion, and parsley very fine. (A food processor works very well for this.) In a large, heavy skillet over medium heat, fry the bacon until it is brown and crisp. When the bacon is cooked, add the olive oil and butter. When the butter is melted, add the chopped vegetables and sauté them for 6 minutes, stirring often to keep them from sticking.

Remove skillet from the heat. Add the Romano cheese, Parmesan cheese, Italian bread crumbs, Tabasco sauce, Worcestershire sauce, salt, black pepper, and lemon juice and stir well. Scoop about 2 tablespoons of the mixture into each tomato half. Place the tomato halves on a lightly greased baking sheet. Bake at 500 degrees until the tops of the tomatoes are nicely browned, about 15 minutes. Serve at once. Serves 10.

Lagniappe: This recipe can be made completely in advance up to the baking of the tomatoes. After you place the tomatoes on the baking sheet, cover them with plastic wrap and refrigerate until you are ready to use. Bake as directed. To freeze, only freeze the stuffing; do not freeze the tomatoes. When you are ready to use, simply thaw the stuffing in the refrigerator or microwave and stuff the tomatoes as directed.

This is an excellent vegetable that can be served as an appetizer. I have also used this stuffing to stuff mushroom caps, squash circles, or bell pepper quarters, and it is excellent. You can also add crabmeat or shrimp to the stuffing at the end of the cooking to make nice appetizers or main dishes. About 194 calories per stuffed tomato half.

BAKED TURNIPS BERNARD

1½ pounds of tender young turnips, finely diced
1 stick of unsalted butter, melted
1 tbsp. of celery, minced
¼ cup of minced onion
1 tsp. of salt

½ tsp. of Tabasco sauce
¼ tsp. of white pepper
¾ cup of heavy cream
½ cup of Ritz cracker crumbs
2 pats of butter, cut into pieces

Preheat the oven to 375 degrees. In a heavy skillet, sauté the turnips in the melted butter for 10 minutes over medium-low heat. Add the celery and onion and sauté for 5 minutes. Add the salt, Tabasco sauce, and white pepper and blend in well. Pour the mixture into a casserole dish and pour the heavy cream over the top. (Do not blend it in.) Sprinkle the top with the cracker crumbs and dot with the butter. Bake at 375 degrees for 30 minutes until the top is golden brown. Serve hot. Serves 4 to 6.

Lagniappe: This dish is best eaten right after it is baked. It does freeze quite well, though. You may also make it up to the baking step, cover it tightly, and store it in the refrigerator until you are ready to bake (up to 24 hours). Or you can bake it completely and store it, tightly covered, in the refrigerator. When you are ready to serve, thaw it in the refrigerator and bake at 300 degrees for 15 minutes, loosely covered. Serve at once. About 328 calories in each of 6 servings and 492 calories in each of 4 servings. No alteration of the recipe is suggested.

Sauces
and
Dressings

CHICKEN PARMESAN SAUCE

2 tbsp. of butter
2 tbsp. of flour
¼ tsp. of salt
¼ tsp. of Tabasco sauce

¾ cup of milk
¼ cup of clear chicken broth
½ cup of grated Parmesan cheese

In a medium saucepan over low heat, melt the butter. Slowly add the flour, stirring constantly. Cook for 3 minutes, but do not let the flour brown. Add the salt and Tabasco sauce and stir in well. Remove from the heat and add the milk and chicken broth. Stir in well. Return to the heat and cook until the sauce thickens. Add the Parmesan cheese and blend well, stirring constantly. Remove from the heat. Serve warm. Makes about 1¾ cups of sauce, enough for 4 chicken breasts.

Lagniappe: This sauce may be made in advance and refrigerated. Heat the sauce in a double boiler or in a small pot placed in a large pot with water in it. Heat the water to a slow boil. Do not let the sauce stick to the sides of the pot.

For a variation, add ½ cup of wine to the sauce and use only ½ cup of milk. Add the wine at the same time that the milk and chicken broth are added. If you divide the sauce into 4 equal servings, there are about 168 calories per serving; about 24 calories per tablespoon or 96 calories per ¼ cup.

CAJUN BARBECUE SAUCE

¼ cup of peanut oil
1 medium onion, finely chopped
2 cloves of garlic, minced
1 stalk of celery, finely minced
½ stick of butter, melted
1 6-ounce can of tomato paste
2 cups of water
1 cup of vinegar
½ cup of dry white wine
2 tbsp. of prepared mustard
½ tsp. of Tabasco sauce
1 tsp. of salt
3 tbsp. of Worcestershire sauce
1 tsp. of white pepper
1 tsp. of freshly ground black pepper
½ tsp. of red pepper
1 tbsp. of paprika
2 tbsp. of sugar
¼ tsp. of cumin
¼ tsp. of filé powder
1 8-ounce can of tomato sauce

In a heavy saucepan, heat the oil over medium heat. Sauté the onion, garlic, and celery until the onions are clear, about 4 minutes. Add the butter and the 6 ounces of tomato paste and simmer over low heat for about 5 minutes. Add the water, vinegar, wine, mustard, Tabasco sauce, salt, and Worcestershire sauce and bring to a boil.

Once the mixture begins to boil, stir it well to make sure it is blended, then reduce the heat to low and add the remaining ingredients. Simmer the sauce for 30 minutes over very low heat. Remove from the heat and cool, then refrigerate until you are ready to use. Use the sauce to baste any barbecue meat that you might cook. Makes about 7 cups of sauce.

Lagniappe: This is a hot barbecue sauce that has multiple uses. You can store it in the refrigerator for about 3 weeks if it is tightly covered. It is a great basting sauce for any meats that you are barbecuing or to add to dishes to make them taste like barbecue (like beans). I find it easiest to make the sauce on the day I know that I am going to barbecue, then use the leftovers as needed later on. About 229 calories per cup or about 14 calories per tablespoon.

BRANDY SAUCE

2 cups of sugar
1 tbsp. of fresh lemon juice
1 stick of butter
2 large eggs, lightly beaten

2 large egg yolks
1 tsp. of vanilla
3 ounces of brandy

In a saucepan over medium heat, heat the sugar and lemon juice, stirring often, until the mixture turns a light brown. In another saucepan over low heat, melt the butter. Remove it from the heat and let it cool, but not solidify.

Using a wire whisk, whip the eggs and egg yolks with the butter until well blended. Add the vanilla and brandy to the melted sugar and mix well. Slowly beat the brandy-sugar mixture into the egg mixture. Return to the stove and heat over low heat until the sauce has thickened. Spoon over Bread Pudding (see recipe) just before serving. Serves 8 to 10.

Lagniappe: This sauce may be made up to 6 hours in advance and reheated over low heat when you are ready to serve. It is also a nice sauce to serve over ice cream for a different kind of treat. About 51 calories per tablespoon or 102 calories per ounce.

HOLLANDAISE SAUCE

1 stick of unsalted butter
4 large egg yolks
2 tbsp. of lemon juice

¼ tsp. of Tabasco sauce
¼ tsp. of salt
1 tsp. of cold water

Melt the butter over low heat and set aside. In a metal mixing bowl, place the egg yolks, lemon juice, Tabasco sauce, salt, and cold water. Using a limber wire whisk, beat the mixture until it is well blended. Boil water in a saucepan that is small enough for the bottom of the metal bowl to rest on top of. When the water is boiling, reduce the heat to simmer (just a little steam should rise) and place the metal bowl on top of the saucepan. Continue to whisk the mixture for about 5 minutes, constantly scraping the sides so that it won't stick or scramble.

When the mixture is thick (like a pudding), slowing add the butter, beating constantly. Make sure that you keep your hand on the bowl. If it gets too hot for you to touch, then it is too hot for the eggs; they'll scramble. If the bowl gets too hot, simply lift it up for a few seconds, then lower it again as it cools. The sauce is ready when the butter is all blended in and the mixture is smooth. Makes about 1 cup of sauce.

Lagniappe: This is a sauce that should be made as it is needed. If you have some left over and don't want to throw it out, store it in the refrigerator in a tightly covered bowl. When you are ready to use it, let it stand at room temperature for about 1 hour, then whip it with a fork. It will regain some of its consistency, and although the flavor will be somewhat altered, the sauce is by no means tasteless.

I also like to use bottled lemon juice in Hollandaise. I know this is a cardinal sin among some cooks, but I prefer the tartness that the bottled lemon juice gives. To each his own! About 66 calories per tablespoon or 265 calories per ¼ cup.

SAUCE RÉMOULADE

3 cloves of garlic
½ cup of chopped fresh parsley (lightly packed)
1 cup of chopped celery
1½ cups of chopped green onion
1 tbsp. of chopped bell pepper
4 tbsp. of Creole mustard
1 tbsp. of Dijon-style mustard
1 tbsp. of horseradish sauce

2 tbsp. of paprika
1 tsp. of salt
½ tsp. of black pepper
½ tsp. of Tabasco sauce
¼ tsp. of white pepper
½ tsp. of onion powder
¼ tsp. of garlic powder
1½ tsp. of sugar
2 tbsp. of red wine vinegar
⅓ cup of vinegar
⅔ cup of quality olive oil

This recipe is easily made in a food processor, or food grinder if you prefer. Chop the garlic in the processor at high speed until it is in very small pieces. Add the parsley and chop again at very high speed, then add the celery and green onion and chop again at high speed until the contents are very well chopped.

Add the bell pepper, Creole mustard, Dijon-style mustard, horseradish sauce, paprika, salt, black pepper, Tabasco sauce, white pepper, onion powder, garlic powder, sugar, and wine vinegar. Blend at high speed until well mixed, about 1 minute. Add the vinegar and blend at high speed for 1 more minute, then slowly drizzle in the olive oil until it is beaten in. Remove from the food processor and refrigerate for 4 to 6 hours. Spoon on top of boiled seafood (shrimp, crabmeat, or crawfish) or serve with raw oysters. Makes about 1 quart of sauce.

Lagniappe: Not only can this sauce be made in advance and refrigerated for up to 3 days, but this storage time seems to improve the flavor. However, do not freeze this sauce. It also makes an excellent salad dressing. To make your boiled seafood look nice, shred a head of lettuce, place the seafood on top, and spoon the sauce over the seafood.

If you make the sauce using a grinder, just grind all the vegetables very fine, mix together using a heavy wire whisk, and beat the olive oil in with the whisk until the sauce has thickened and blended. Use this sauce to make **Shrimp Rémoulade, Crawfish Rémoulade, Crabmeat Rémoulade,** and **Oysters Rémoulade.** About 24 calories per tablespoon or 94 calories per ¼ cup.

HOT DIPPING SAUCE FOR SEAFOOD

1 cup of catsup
1 cup of mayonnaise
1 tbsp. of Tabasco sauce

2 tbsp. of fresh lemon juice
1 tbsp. of Worcestershire sauce

Mix all of the ingredients and let stand for 1 hour to blend the flavors fully. Makes about 2¼ cups of sauce.

Lagniappe: This is a quick and easy sauce for boiled crawfish or shrimp that can be made 24 hours in advance. It is easy, but excellent. About 212 calories per ¼ cup or 53 calories per tablespoon.

COCKTAIL SAUCE FOR SEAFOOD

1 cup of catsup
½ cup of chili sauce
3 tbsp. of horseradish sauce
1 tsp. of Tabasco sauce
¼ cup of minced celery
1 clove of garlic, minced
2 green onions, minced

1 tbsp. of minced fresh parsley
1 tsp. of salt
1 tbsp. of Worcestershire sauce
¼ tsp. of sweet basil
1 bay leaf, crushed
2 tbsp. of fresh lemon juice

Mix all of the ingredients and let stand for 3 hours, tightly covered, in the refrigerator. Makes about 2 cups of sauce.

Lagniappe: You can make this up to 3 days in advance for use as needed. It is an excellent sauce for any seafood—shrimp, crawfish, crabs, or oysters. Use as a dipping sauce or spoon it over the cooked seafood. About 61 calories per ¼ cup or 15½ calories per tablespoon.

CRABMEAT DRESSING

¼ stick of unsalted butter
1 small onion, diced
¼ cup of diced bell pepper
1 stalk of celery, diced
2 cloves of garlic, minced
1 pound of fresh lump crabmeat
½ tsp. of Tabasco sauce
1 tsp. of salt
¼ tsp. of white pepper
¼ tsp. of black pepper

1 tsp. of Worcestershire sauce
1 tbsp. of fresh lemon juice
2½ cups of diced fresh French bread
½ cup of milk
3 tbsp. of diced pimento
¼ cup of minced fresh parsley
½ cup of finely chopped green onion tops

In a large skillet, melt the butter over medium heat. Sauté the onion, bell pepper, celery, and garlic for 5 minutes. Add the crabmeat, Tabasco sauce, salt, white pepper, black pepper, Worcestershire sauce, and lemon juice. Blend and sauté until ingredients are well mixed, but be careful not to tear up the lump crabmeat.

Soak the French bread in the milk for 2 minutes, then squeeze the bread with your hands to remove most of the milk. Add the bread to the crab mixture. Reduce the heat to low and add the pimento, parsley, and green onion tops. Cook for 5 minutes, lightly turning the mixture a few times to prevent it from sticking. Remove from the heat.

Serve hot as a side dish or in any dish that calls for stuffing (such as Veal De Ridder—see index for recipe). Makes about 5 cups of dressing.

Lagniappe: This is a versatile stuffing or dressing. Use it on top of your favorite baked or fried fish fillets, on top of fried pork, or on top of broiled beef. It can be served by itself in individual serving dishes; just dust it with some bread crumbs or cracker crumbs, dot it with butter, and bake for 15 minutes at 300 degrees.

It can be made in advance and refrigerated, but it loses freshness and quality. Do not freeze this dish; it does not freeze well at all. About 205 calories per cup or 52 calories per ¼ cup.

OYSTER DRESSING

½ cup of butter
1 medium onion, chopped
½ medium bell pepper, finely chopped
1 stalk of celery, chopped
2 cloves of garlic, minced
1 loaf of French bread
water to soak bread
½ tsp. of Tabasco sauce

2 pints of oysters, cut in half and drained (reserve liquor)
1½ tsp. of Chicken Seasoning Mix (see index for recipe)
½ cup of chopped green onion
¼ cup of finely chopped fresh parsley

Melt the butter in a large skillet over medium heat. Sauté the onion, bell pepper, celery, and garlic until they are limp, about 3 minutes. Tear the French bread into pieces and soak it in water to soften.

While the bread is soaking, add the Tabasco sauce, oysters, Chicken Seasoning Mix, green onion, and parsley to the skillet and sauté for 2 minutes. Remove the bread from the water and squeeze out the excess water with your hands. Add the bread and ¼ cup of the reserved oyster liquor to the skillet. Cook for 5 minutes over medium-low heat, stirring constantly. Serve hot as a stuffing or dressing. Serves 8 to 10.

Lagniappe: This dressing can be used to stuff chicken, duck, turkey, fish, or pork chops. You can also stuff bell peppers with it. It makes an excellent dish; just top with bread crumbs, dot with butter, and bake for 10 minutes at 350 degrees. Eight servings have about 311 calories each, and 10 servings have about 249 calories each.

CHICKEN-TURNIP DRESSING

4 large tender turnips (about 2 pounds)
water to steam turnips
2 strips of bacon, chopped
2 tbsp. of unsalted butter
1 pound of chicken breasts, deboned and diced
1½ tsp. of Chicken Seasoning Mix (see index for recipe)
1 large onion, diced
1 medium bell pepper, chopped
1 stalk of celery, minced

3 cloves of garlic, minced
½ tsp. of Tabasco sauce
¼ tsp. of black pepper
¼ tsp. of garlic powder
1 cup of Ritz cracker crumbs
1 cup of cooked white rice
½ cup of chopped green onion
½ cup of minced fresh parsley
½ cup of Chicken Stock (see index for recipe) or chicken broth

Wash the turnips, place them in a steamer, and steam them for 15 minutes. Let them cool, then dice and set aside for later use.

In a heavy skillet, sauté the bacon over medium heat until it is brown and crisp. Add the butter and stir until it is melted. Season the diced chicken with the Chicken Seasoning Mix and sauté in the butter-bacon mixture until it is cooked, about 5 minutes. Add the diced turnips, onion, bell pepper, celery, and garlic and sauté for 5 minutes. Add the remaining ingredients and mix well. Serve right from the pot or pour into a casserole dish and bake at 350 degrees for 15 minutes. Serve hot. Serves 6.

Lagniappe: This dish may be made in advance and frozen for later use or stored in the refrigerator for up to 3 days. To reheat, just thaw in the refrigerator if frozen and bake at 350 degrees for 20 minutes. Good as a side dish, but the dressing is also very nice when used to stuff a hen or a goose. About 288 calories per serving.

EGGPLANT DRESSING

1 large eggplant, diced
1 large onion, chopped
1 medium bell pepper, chopped
2 stalks of celery, chopped
4 cloves of garlic, minced
2 tbsp. of butter
1 pound of ground chuck
1 cup of chopped boiled shrimp
1½ tsp. of Beef Seasoning Mix (see index for recipe)
1 tbsp. of Worcestershire sauce
½ tsp. of Tabasco sauce
½ tsp. of onion powder
¼ tsp. of garlic powder
½ tsp. of freshly ground black pepper
½ cup of minced green onion
¼ cup of minced fresh parsley
2 cups of cooked white rice
¼ cup of bread crumbs

In a large skillet, sauté the eggplant, onion, bell pepper, celery, and garlic in the butter until tender, about 10 to 12 minutes. Add the ground chuck and cook until it is well browned. Preheat the oven to 350 degrees. Add the shrimp, Beef Seasoning Mix, Worcestershire sauce, Tabasco sauce, onion powder, garlic powder, and black pepper and sauté for 3 minutes. Add the green onion, parsley, and rice and mix well. Pour into a casserole dish and sprinkle the top with the bread crumbs. Bake for 15 minutes at 350 degrees. Serve hot. Serves 6.

Lagniappe: This is a quick and easy dressing that you can serve as a side dish with almost any meal. It can be made in advance and frozen or refrigerated. To reheat, just thaw in the refrigerator if frozen and bake for 20 minutes at 350 degrees.

An alternate serving suggestion: instead of peeling the eggplant, scoop out the meat from the center, leaving a nice eggplant boat. Make the dressing, stuff it into the shell, and bake as directed. It makes a nice main dish served this way and also improves the looks of the dish. About 292 calories per serving.

Sweets

OATMEAL COOKIES

½ cup of shortening
¼ cup of unsalted butter
1 cup of sugar
¼ cup of light brown sugar
2 large eggs, beaten
1 cup of flour
1 tsp. of baking powder
¼ tsp. of baking soda
¼ tsp. of ginger

½ tsp. of cinnamon
¼ tsp. of ground cloves
½ tsp. of nutmeg
½ tsp. of salt
½ cup of milk
3 cups of old-fashioned oats
½ cup of raisins
¾ cup of chopped pecans
butter to grease baking sheet

Preheat the oven to 375 degrees. Cream the shortening, butter, sugar, and brown sugar in a large mixing bowl until completely blended. Add the eggs and beat them in well. Mix the flour, baking powder, baking soda, ginger, cinnamon, cloves, nutmeg, and salt in another mixing bowl. Add this mixture to the sugar mixture about ¼ cup at a time alternately with about ¼ of the milk at a time, mixing after each addition. Mix the oats, raisins, and pecans and pour this mixture into the batter, blending it in very well.

Drop the batter by tablespoonfuls on lightly greased baking sheets. Bake at 375 degrees for about 12 minutes or until the cookies are brown around the edges and somewhat firm in the center. Let the cookies cool before you take them off the baking sheet or serve them. This recipe makes about 3½ dozen cookies.

Lagniappe: You can make this dough in advance and refrigerate it for a while before use, or you can freeze the cookies after they are baked. They also keep well in an airtight cookie jar. About 112 calories per cookie.

SUGAR COOKIES

1 cup of butter
⅔ cup of sugar
1 large egg
2 tsp. of vanilla

3 cups of flour
1 tsp. of baking powder
¼ tsp. of salt
⅛ tsp. of nutmeg

Preheat the oven to 350 degrees. In a large mixing bowl, cream the butter and sugar together until very creamy. Add the egg and vanilla and blend with an electric mixer at high speed until the mixture is fluffy. Mix together the flour, baking powder, salt, and nutmeg. Blend in with the butter mixture gradually. The dough will be stiff and somewhat tacky.

Lightly flour a cutting board and roll small amounts of dough out, about ¼ inch thick. Cut with your favorite cookie cutters or with biscuit cutters. Bake on ungreased cookie sheets at 350 degrees for about 10 minutes. Depending on the size of your cutters, this recipe will make about 3 dozen cookies.

Lagniappe: The dough may be made in advance and stored in the refrigerator until you are ready to use it. You can sprinkle powdered sugar lightly on the tops of the cookies as they are cooling for a nice effect. Each cookie has about 104 calories.

BOURBON BALLS

1 cup of fine vanilla wafer crumbs
1 cup of fine graham cracker crumbs
2 cups of powdered sugar
2 cups of chopped pecans
3½ tbsp. of cocoa
¼ cup of light corn syrup
¾ cup of bourbon
½ cup of sugar

Combine the vanilla wafer crumbs, graham cracker crumbs, powdered sugar, pecans, and cocoa and mix well. Add the corn syrup and bourbon and mix well. Shape into 1-inch balls and roll the balls in the sugar. Store in a tightly covered container for at least 48 hours. Makes about 40 balls.

Lagniappe: You can make these up to 1 week in advance and store them in an airtight container. They are excellent. About 106 calories per ball. Don't look to count calories in this recipe. It is delicious, but you pay for it!

PRALINES

4 cups of sugar
½ cup of light brown sugar
½ cup of water
1 cup of evaporated milk

1 stick of butter
½ tsp. of salt
4 cups of pecan pieces
1½ tsp. of vanilla

Mix the sugar, brown sugar, water, evaporated milk, butter, and salt in a medium-size heavy saucepan and bring to a boil over medium heat. When the mixture begins to boil, reduce the heat to low and cook, stirring constantly, until a soft ball forms when a small amount of the mixture is dropped into cold water. Add the pecans and cook for 4 more minutes.

Remove from the heat and beat in the vanilla for 1 minute, then drop about 2 tablespoonfuls at a time onto a buttered platter or waxed paper. Let the pralines harden, then store in a tightly covered container in a cool place. Makes about 40 pralines.

Lagniappe: Pralines will easily keep a week without any loss of texture or flavor. Do not freeze. An excellent candy or dessert. Each praline has about 198 calories.

OREILLES DE COCHON

½ stick of unsalted butter
2 large eggs, beaten
2 cups of flour
1½ tsp. of baking powder
½ tsp. of salt

cooking oil for deep-frying
2 cups of cane syrup
1 tbsp. of molasses
1 cup of chopped pecans

Mix the butter and eggs in a bowl. Combine the flour, baking powder, and salt in another bowl. Slowly, about ½ cup at a time, add the flour to the butter mixture, stirring after each addition. The dough will be easy to handle.

Separate the dough into 16 1-inch balls. On a lightly floured surface, roll each of the balls into a thin circle about 4 to 6 inches in diameter. Pour about 3 inches of oil into a deep fryer and heat the oil to about 350 degrees. Fry the circles one at a time. Using a fork, twist one side of the circle with a fork to give it a swirl and make it look somewhat like a pig's ear. When the "ear" is light brown, remove and drain on a paper towel. Repeat the process until all the ears are fried. Set them aside while you make the topping.

In a small saucepan over medium heat, cook the syrup and molasses until the syrup reaches the soft ball stage. Add the pecans and cook for 2 more minutes. Drizzle the topping over the ears and serve either warm or cool. An excellent dessert or snack. Makes about 16 large cakes.

Lagniappe: This is an old Acadian treat. *Oreilles de cochon,* of course, is Cajun French for "pigs' ears." You can make the oreilles one or two days in advance. Just keep them tightly covered in a cool place. There are about 286 calories per cake.

CHEESE CAKE

1 recipe of Graham Cracker Crust (see next recipe)

3 pounds of cream cheese, softened

6 large brown eggs, lightly beaten

juice of 2 lemons

1¾ cups of sugar

4½ tbsp. of vanilla

¼ tsp. of nutmeg

⅛ tsp. of cinnamon

Preheat the oven to 350 degrees. Mold crust onto the sides and bottom of a large springform cake pan. Bake at 350 degrees for 5 minutes, then remove from the oven and let it cool. Put the remaining ingredients into a large mixing bowl and beat with an electric mixer at medium-high speed until the mixture is very smooth.

Raise the oven temperature to 400 degrees. Pour the batter into the cake pan and place the pan in the oven when the temperature has reached 400 degrees. Bake for 20 minutes, then lower the temperature to 300 degrees and bake for another 20 minutes. Lower the temperature to 250 degrees and bake until the cake has set, about 1 hour and 15 minutes. Remove from the oven and cool before serving. Serves 12 to 15.

Lagniappe: You can make and store this cake in the refrigerator for a few days. You can also decorate the cake by adding the fruit topping of your choice. I have frozen this cheese cake, and although its texture is fair and its taste is not altered, I find that the quality is affected. But if you insist on freezing, defrost in the refrigerator until ready to serve.

If you cut it into 12 slices, figure about 776 calories per slice; if you cut 15 slices, figure about 621 calories per serving. If you want to reduce calories in this cake, all you can do is cut yourself a smaller piece!

GRAHAM CRACKER CRUST

3 cups of graham cracker crumbs
½ cup of melted butter

¼ cup of sugar
2 tbsp. of light brown sugar

In a large mixing bowl, mix all the ingredients until well blended. Mold the cracker crumb mixture to the sides and bottom of the pie pan or springform pan with your fingers. Use as a shell for pies or cakes.

Lagniappe: I find that the easiest way to mix this crust is to put all the ingredients into my food processor and blend at full speed for 1 minute, then mold as above. About 2,319 calories in the whole crust.

LOUISIANA PEAR CAKE

1½ cups of cooking oil
2 cups of sugar
¼ cup of light brown sugar
3 eggs, lightly beaten
2½ cups of flour
2 tsp. of baking powder
1 tsp. of baking soda
1 tsp. of salt
2 tsp. of nutmeg

1½ tsp. of cinnamon
¼ tsp. of ginger
¼ tsp. of orange peel spice
3 cups of diced canning
    pears, peeled and cored
1 cup of chopped pecans
2 tsp. of vanilla
butter and flour for cake pan
powdered sugar to dust cake

Preheat the oven to 350 degrees. Cream the oil, sugar, and brown sugar in a bowl until well mixed. Add the eggs and mix well. In another bowl, mix the flour, baking powder, baking soda, salt, nutmeg, cinnamon, ginger, and orange peel; blend well. In another bowl, combine the pears and pecans.

Blend the pear mixture with the flour mixture and slowly add this to the sugar mixture, mixing well. Blend the vanilla in well. Pour into a lightly greased and floured bundt cake pan and bake for 1 hour at 350 degrees. Remove from the oven and cool, then sprinkle with powdered sugar. Serves 10.

Lagniappe: This is a very moist cake that will keep for almost a whole week. Keep it covered. You can also make muffins with this recipe; just pour into muffin tins and bake for 20 minutes at 350 degrees. You can also use this recipe to make **Fresh Apple Cake** by substituting 3 cups of apples. Leave the peelings on and cut out the cores. I like to use 1 cup of bitter green apple and 2 cups of red apple; it makes a nice combination. Around 739 calories per serving.

WEST FORK CAJUN CAKE

2 large eggs
1½ cups of sugar
1 20-ounce can of crushed
  pineapple
2 cups of flour
2 tbsp. of baking soda
½ tsp. of salt

butter to grease baking dish
1 stick of butter
¼ cup of sugar
1 5.33-ounce can of
  evaporated milk
1 cup of shredded coconut
2 cups of chopped pecans

Preheat the oven to 350 degrees. In a large mixing bowl, beat the eggs well. Add the 1½ cups of sugar and beat until creamed. Add the pineapple and blend in. In another bowl, mix the flour, baking soda, and salt until well mixed. Slowly add the flour mixture to the egg mixture about ¼ at a time, mixing in well after each addition.

Pour batter into a well-greased 9 by 13 baking dish. Bake at 350 degrees for 35 minutes. Remove from oven and allow to cool. Leave the cake in the baking dish. In a medium saucepan over medium heat, melt the stick of butter. Add the ¼ cup of sugar, evaporated milk, coconut, and pecans and reduce the heat to low. Cook over low heat for 12 minutes, stirring constantly. Pour this mixture over the cooled cake and spread it evenly. Allow the cake to cool for 30 minutes before cutting. Serves 10 to 12.

Lagniappe: This cake can be made up to 24 hours before serving. It stays very fresh because the icing seals the moisture into the cake. It is excellent with coffee or as a dessert. This recipe originated at a small fishing camp on the West Fork of the Calcasieu River, about 22 miles from Lake Charles. About 629 calories per serving in 10 servings and about 524 calories per serving in 12 servings.

This recipe is from my brother, Guy G. Theriot of Lake Charles.

SYRUP CAKE

1 stick of unsalted butter
1 cup of sugar
¼ cup of dark brown sugar
3 large eggs, slightly beaten
2 cups of cane syrup
1 cup of evaporated milk
4 cups of flour

1½ tsp. of baking powder
1 tsp. of baking soda
½ tsp. of salt
1 tsp. of cinnamon
1 tsp. of nutmeg
½ tsp. of cloves
¼ tsp. of lemon peel spice

Preheat the oven to 350 degrees. Cream the butter, sugar, and brown sugar well. Add the eggs, cane syrup, and evaporated milk. In another bowl, mix the flour, baking powder, baking soda, salt, cinnamon, nutmeg, cloves, and lemon peel. Add about ¼ of the flour mixture at a time to the butter-sugar mixture, mixing well after each addition.

Pour into a 9 by 13 cake pan and bake for 30 to 40 minutes or until a toothpick inserted into the center of the cake comes out clean. Serve right from the oven or cool and serve. Serves 12.

Lagniappe: This cake keeps well if you keep it covered. You can make it up to 3 days in advance. I have also frozen it with good results; just wrap it tightly before freezing. Let it thaw in the pan, covered, at room temperature. A good coffee cake, snack cake, or dessert. Great eating at about 504 calories per serving.

FRESH COCONUT CAKE

½ stick of unsalted butter
1 tbsp. of flour
3 cups of fresh grated coconut
1 13-ounce can of evaporated milk
2 cups of sugar
1½ tbsp. of light corn syrup
1 tsp. of vanilla

1 recipe of Yellow Layer Cake (see next recipe) or any 2 9-inch yellow layer cakes
1 recipe of White Cake Frosting (see index for recipe)
¼ cup of fresh grated coconut

Melt the butter in a medium saucepan over medium heat. Add the flour and blend it in well. Cook for 3 minutes, then add the 3 cups of coconut and cook for 2 minutes. Add the evaporated milk, sugar, and corn syrup and cook until the mixture thickens. Remove from the heat and beat in the vanilla.

Spread the mixture between the cake layers and on top of the top layer. Cover the top and sides of the cake with White Cake Frosting and sprinkle with the ¼ cup of coconut. Serve at once or let the filling cool. Serves 10.

Lagniappe: This cake can be made a day or even 2 days in advance and will still keep a great deal of moisture because it is well sealed by the frosting. A real treat! About 855 calories per serving. To reduce calories, you can only cut yourself a smaller slice of cake.

YELLOW LAYER CAKE

½ cup of vegetable
  shortening
1½ cups of sugar
2 large eggs
1 tsp. of vanilla
2 cups of all-purpose flour

2½ tsp. of baking powder
½ tsp. of baking soda
1 tsp. of salt
1 cup of milk
1 tbsp. of water
butter and flour for cake pans

Preheat the oven to 375 degrees. In a large mixing bowl, cream the shortening until it is soft and fluffy. Add the sugar ½ cup at a time, creaming thoroughly after each addition. Add the eggs and vanilla and beat well until mixture is well blended and smooth. In another mixing bowl, combine the flour, baking powder, baking soda, and salt and mix well. Add ⅓ of the flour mixture at a time to the sugar mixture alternately with ⅓ of the milk at a time, blending well after each addition. Add the water and blend until the batter is smooth and light.

Pour into two greased and floured 9-inch cake pans. Bake at 375 degrees for 25 minutes or until a toothpick inserted into the middle of the cakes comes out clean. Let cakes cool before you remove them from their pans.

Lagniappe: This is a plain cake that may be served as is or with one of the frostings found in this section. It may also be sprinkled with a little powdered sugar or brown sugar and served as a coffee cake. Each layer of the cake has about 1,701 calories.

WHITE CAKE FROSTING

1½ cups of sugar
3 tbsp. of light corn syrup
¼ cup of water

4 egg whites
½ tsp. of cream of tartar
1 tbsp. of vanilla

In a small saucepan over medium heat, combine the sugar, corn syrup, and water. Cook until the mixture thickens and a drop put into a cup of cold water forms a hard ball.

Beat the egg whites until stiff. Add the cream of tartar and vanilla. Slowly drizzle the hot sugar mixture into the beaten egg whites, beating constantly. The frosting should stand in stiff peaks. Spread on either a cool or warm cake. Frosts a two- or three-layer cake.

Lagniappe: You can't make this in advance; make it just after you take the layers from the oven. It spreads well over cool or warm cake and does a great job of keeping the cake from drying out. This frosting will add about 1,593 calories to your cake.

PECAN CAKE FROSTING

1 stick of butter
1 cup of sugar
2 cups of light brown sugar
2 tbsp. of evaporated milk

2 tbsp. of all-purpose flour
4 egg yolks, well beaten
1½ cups of pecan pieces
1 tsp. of vanilla

In a large saucepan, melt the butter. Add the sugar, brown sugar, evaporated milk, flour, and egg yolks. Cook for 5 minutes over low heat. Add ½ cup of the pecans and cook for 2 minutes. Remove from the heat and add the vanilla and the remaining pecans. Allow the mixture to cool for 2 minutes, then spread evenly on cake. Frosts two 9-inch layer cakes.

Lagniappe: This is an excellent cake topping. You can do other things with it, like add ½ to 1 cup of coconut with the pecans to make a topping for German chocolate cake. It can also be used on top of a sheet cake to make an excellent coffee cake. This frosting will add about 4,372 calories to a cake.

BREAD PUDDING

15 slices of bread or 1 loaf of French bread
1 13-ounce can of evaporated milk
2½ cups of milk
1 stick of butter, cut into pieces
5 eggs, well beaten
2 cups of sugar
1 Granny Smith apple, peeled and diced
1 10-ounce package frozen sweetened peaches, chopped
½ cup of raisins
½ cup of chopped pecans
1 tsp. of allspice
1 tsp. of nutmeg
1½ tsp. of cinnamon
1 tbsp. of vanilla
butter to grease pudding pan
water for baking pan
Brandy Sauce (optional—see index for recipe)

Preheat the oven to 350 degrees. Tear the bread into pieces and place in a large glass bowl. In a saucepan over low heat, combine the evaporated milk, milk, and butter. Heat until the butter is melted and the milk is hot. Pour over the bread and mix well. Let stand for 10 minutes, then add the eggs, sugar, apple, peaches, raisins, and pecans. Blend well. Add the allspice, nutmeg, cinnamon, and vanilla. Mix very well.

Pour into a lightly greased ovenproof 9 by 13 pan and set this pan into a baking pan with 1 inch of water in it. Bake at 350 degrees for about 1 hour or until a knife inserted into the center comes out clean. Allow to cool for 15 minutes, then serve hot or cold with Brandy Sauce if desired. (The sauce is best heated a bit.) Serves 8 to 10.

Lagniappe: You can make this bread pudding 2 or 3 days in advance. Heat it in individual servings by placing it under the broiler for 2 minutes or by heating it in the microwave at 80 percent power for 1 minute. It can be frozen, but the texture is somewhat affected. I would suggest refrigerating it instead. It is also wonderful just from the oven with plenty of warm Brandy Sauce.

About 763 calories per serving in 8 servings without the sauce or 865 calories per serving with 2 tablespoons of sauce. In 10 servings, there are about 611 calories per serving without the sauce or 713 calories with 2 tablespoons of sauce.

CAJUN RICE CUSTARD

2 cups of milk
1¼ cups of sugar
¼ cup of packed light brown sugar
4 large brown eggs, lightly beaten
1 medium apple, diced
½ cup of raisins

½ cup of crushed pineapple
¼ tsp. of ginger
½ tsp. of nutmeg
¼ tsp. of cinnamon
1 cup of cooked white rice
water for baking pan
2 cups of freshly whipped cream (optional)

Pour the milk into a heavy saucepan and bring to a boil over medium heat. Reduce the heat to low and simmer until the milk is scalded. Mix the sugar, brown sugar, and eggs until well creamed. Add the milk to the sugar mixture and blend in well. Add the apple, raisins, pineapple, ginger, nutmeg, cinnamon, and rice and blend until well mixed.

Pour into a shallow 2½-quart baking dish and place the dish in a large baking pan with 1 inch of water in it. Bake at 325 degrees for 1 hour or until a knife inserted into the center comes out clean. Remove from the oven and let cool for 15 to 20 minutes or refrigerate. Serve warm or cool with a nice helping of fresh whipped cream if you like. Serves 8 to 12.

Lagniappe: Do not freeze. You can bake this custard ahead of time and refrigerate it until you are ready to serve. It will keep in the refrigerator for about 3 days. Serve it cold or heat it up in the oven at 300 degrees for about 5 to 7 minutes and serve it warm. Individual servings also heat up well in the microwave at 70 percent power for about 30 seconds. The calories are as follows: in 8 servings—about 385 calories per serving; in 10 servings—about 308 calories per serving; and in 12 servings— about 257 calories per serving (all with whipped cream).

CREAM CUSTARD

12 tbsp. of dark brown sugar
5 large eggs, beaten
2 cups of half-and-half
½ cup of milk
½ cup of water
½ cup of light brown sugar

⅓ cup of dark brown sugar
3 tsp. of vanilla
¼ tsp. of nutmeg
⅛ tsp. of salt
water for baking pan

Distribute the 12 tablespoons of dark brown sugar evenly among 8 6-ounce custard cups (1½ tablespoons sprinkled in each). Press the sugar down with your fingers so that it is somewhat packed.

Preheat the oven to 350 degrees. In a large mixing bowl beat the eggs, half-and-half, milk, and water with a wire whisk until smooth and somewhat frothy. Add the light brown sugar, the ⅓ cup of dark brown sugar, vanilla, nutmeg, and salt and beat with the whisk until all the sugar has dissolved.

Pour this mixture equally into the custard cups and set the cups in a large shallow baking pan that has about 1 inch of water in it. Bake at 350 degrees for 45 to 55 minutes or until a knife placed just inside the rim of a custard cup comes out clean. Remove from the oven and allow the custard to cool.

When you are ready to serve, run a knife around the inside edge of each cup to assist you in unmolding. Hold a small saucer upside down over the top of the cup, then invert the cup. The custard should fall onto the saucer and the melted brown sugar should fall around the top, sides, and base. Serve warm from the oven or cold. Serves 8.

Lagniappe: This is an excellent light dessert. You can make the custard the day before you need it and cover the top of the custard with either plastic wrap or aluminum foil to keep food odors out. Do *not* freeze this dessert! If you make it in advance and would like to serve it slightly warm, place the custard (still in the cups) back in the shallow pan, fill the pan with boiling water, and let the custard sit until the water has cooled. Then unmold the custard and serve. About 307 calories per serving.

PAIN PERDU
(FRENCH TOAST)

2 large eggs, well beaten
¾ cup of milk
½ cup of sugar
½ tsp. of cinnamon
½ tsp. of nutmeg

⅛ tsp. of salt
½ tsp. of fresh lemon juice
8 slices of stale bread
2 tbsp. of peanut oil

In a large bowl, mix the eggs, milk, sugar, cinnamon, nutmeg, salt, and lemon juice. Beat well with a wire whisk or fork for about 1 minute. Place the bread in the bowl, a slice at a time, and let the bread soak up the egg mixture on each side.

Heat the oil in a heavy metal skillet over medium-low heat until it is hot. Fry each slice of bread until it has browned nicely on each side. Serve warm right from the skillet or, if you like, sprinkled with powdered sugar or topped with syrup. Serves 4.

Lagniappe: Pain perdu ("lost bread") is the Lousiana version of French toast. Do not make it in advance; prepare just before you are ready to serve. It is possible to freeze pain perdu, but I am not thrilled with the results and it is really so easy to make when you feel like having some. A great breakfast dish! Only about 366 calories per serving (2 slices).

PRUNE BREAD

4 cups of all-purpose flour
1 tsp. of baking powder
1 tsp. of baking soda
1 pound of dried prunes
1¾ cups of warm water
2 cups of sugar
¼ cup of dark brown sugar
2 large eggs, beaten

1 tsp. of salt
¾ cup of shortening
1 tsp. of nutmeg
¼ tsp. of ginger
½ tsp. of cinnamon
½ tsp. of cloves
¼ tsp. of lemon peel spice
butter and flour for loaf pans

Preheat the oven to 350 degrees. Mix the flour, baking powder, and baking soda in a large bowl. Cut the prunes into small pieces and combine them with the warm water. Mix the prunes and water with the sugar, brown sugar, eggs, salt, and shortening until well mixed. Mix the nutmeg, ginger, cinnamon, cloves, and lemon peel into the flour mixture. Add the flour mixture to the prune mixture about ¼ at a time until well blended.

Pour equally into 2 lightly greased and floured 9 by 5 by 3 loaf pans. Bake at 350 degrees for 1 hour or until a toothpick inserted into the center comes out clean. Serve at room temperature. Each loaf serves 8 to 10.

Lagniappe: You can make this recipe and freeze one of the loaves for later use. To use, just thaw at room temperature in a covered cake dish or plastic cake pan. It is also excellent slightly heated and served with fresh butter. About 825 calories per serving in 8 servings and about 660 calories per serving in 10 servings.

DATE NUT BREAD

1½ cups of pecan halves
1 pound of whole pitted
  dates
1 cup of all-purpose flour
2 tsp. of baking powder
½ tsp. of baking soda
½ tsp. of salt

¼ tsp. of orange peel
  seasoning
5 egg yolks
¾ cup of sugar
½ cup of dark corn syrup
5 egg whites, stiffly beaten
1½ tsp. of vanilla
butter and flour for pan

Preheat the oven to 325 degrees. In a mixing bowl, mix the pecans, dates, flour, baking powder, baking soda, salt, and orange peel. Be sure to coat the pecans and dates well with the flour so they will not all sink to the bottom of the pan during baking. In another bowl, beat the egg yolks with the sugar and corn syrup until very creamy. Combine this mixture with the pecan-date mixture until well blended. Fold in the egg whites and vanilla.

Pour the mixture into a well greased and floured loaf pan or tube pan and bake at 325 degrees for 1 hour or until a toothpick inserted into the center comes out clean. Let the bread cool and remove it from the pan. Serve in slices. Serves 12.

Lagniappe: This bread is excellent served as your bread at mealtime or served with coffee anytime. It may also be baked as muffins for breakfast; pour dough into muffin tins and bake for 25 to 30 minutes, testing with a toothpick for doneness. The bread freezes well; just let it thaw at room temperature in a covered cake plate or covered with plastic wrap so it won't dry out. About 363 calories per serving.

BANANA NUT BREAD

2 medium bananas, peeled
1 tsp. of lemon juice
2 eggs, beaten
1 cup of milk
2½ cups of flour
1½ cups of sugar
¼ cup of dark brown sugar
¼ tsp. of salt
3 tsp. of baking powder
½ tsp. of nutmeg
1 tsp. of vanilla
½ cup of chopped black walnuts
flour for loaf pan

Preheat the oven to 350 degrees. Mash the bananas well in a bowl with a fork. Add the lemon juice to the bananas and mix well. Mix the eggs and milk in another bowl. Mix the flour, sugar, brown sugar, salt, baking powder, and nutmeg in another bowl. Mix ⅓ of the flour mixture with the egg-milk mixture until well mixed. Add the vanilla. Mix in ⅓ more of the flour mixture until well mixed. Mix the black walnuts with the remaining flour mixture and add this to the batter, mixing well. Add the bananas and mix until smooth.

Pour into a floured 9 by 5 by 3 loaf pan. Bake at 350 degrees for 50 minutes to 1 hour or until a toothpick inserted into the center of the bread comes out clean. Let cool for 5 minutes before cutting. Serves 8 to 12.

Lagniappe: You can bake this bread and freeze it for later use. Just thaw at room temperature in a covered cake plate, then serve as desired. It is nice to put a few up in the freezer and take one out when you expect company. The calories for this recipe are as follows: in 8 servings—about 436 calories per serving; in 10 servings—about 349 calories per serving; and in 12 servings—about 291 calories per serving.